HIDDEN VICTORY

In 1941 a battle as significant to the war in Europe as the Battle of Britain was won against the Iraqi Army and Air Force by No. 4 Flying Training School at Habbaniya.

In 1991 a famous war-artist, the late Frank Wootton, read about the battle and was upset that almost no one in Britain had heard about it. He decided to paint a memorial picture and chose to create a scene using events that had occurred from about nine o'clock on the first morning of the battle. A photograph of his picture appears above.

To the left is the plateau on which the enemy Iraqis were dug in, overlooking the RAF camp and the river Euphrates. On the right are the School's silver Audaxes starting to dive-bomb. Some of the Iraqi elements are already on fire, having been struck earlier. In the centre are yellow Oxfords doing level-bombing. The one marked 'D' is flown by Tony Dudgeon. Black puffs of light anti-aircraft fire can be seen; one of the Oxfords has been hit and set on fire – its three crewmen will be killed in the ensuing crash. On the airfield, seen below the Oxfords, is a Wellington which had to force land; within minutes it had been shelled by the Iraqis, set on fire and its bombs are now exploding. In the centre background, by the hangars, another Oxford is burning after being shelled.

The School's losses were grave; it lost a quarter of its effectiveness and a third of its aircraft in the first fourteen hours. However, after five days and four nights of this maximum Air Force effort the Iraqi Army fled, routed, and did not fight any further battle before surrendering three weeks later.

Marshal of the RAF Lord Tedder, Commander-in-Chief of all the air Forces in the Middle East, said in 1943, in Algiers: '…it is a Royal Air Force epic. If the School had been overcome,…the whole course of the European war would have been changed drastically, if we had not lost it altogether.'

HIDDEN VICTORY

The Battle of Habbaniya, May 1941

Air Vice-Marshal A.G. Dudgeon, CBE, DFC

TEMPUS

First published 2000

PUBLISHED IN THE UNITED KINGDOM BY:

Tempus Publishing Ltd
The Mill, Brimscombe Port
Stroud, Gloucestershire GL5 2QG

PUBLISHED IN THE UNITED STATES OF AMERICA BY:

Tempus Publishing Inc.
2 Cumberland Street
Charleston, SC 29401

Tempus books are available in France, Germany and Belgium
from the following addresses:

Tempus Publishing Group	Tempus Publishing Group	Tempus Publishing Group
21 Avenue de la République	Gustav-Adolf-Straße 3	Place de L'Alma 4/5
37300 Joué-lès-Tours	99084 Erfurt	1200 Brussels
FRANCE	GERMANY	BELGIUM

British Library Cataloguing in Publication Data.
A catalogue record for this book is available from the British Library.

ISBN 0 7524 2001 1

Typesetting and origination by Tempus Publishing.
PRINTED AND BOUND IN GREAT BRITAIN.

To the 'Forgotten Few'
Officers, NCOs, Airmen and Pupils of No. 4 Flying Training School
who, in May 1941, won a crucial victory against the Iraqi Army and Air Force but
received no commendation for their success.

also

To my four grandchildren
Pip, Mel, Nix, Gems

Contents

Preface		xiii
German Map		x–xi
1	Germany Ascendant: 1941	1
2	The Crisis and The Historians	5
3	Gunboat Diplomats	10
4	Iraq: 1920 to 1941	17
5	Air Vice-Marshal Smart	23
6	Preparations	33
7	Coming to the Boil	47
8	The Battle: Day 1	57
9	Enemy Reactions	83
10	The Battle: Days 2-6	86
11	Germany Moves	101
12	Clearing Up: Days 7-15	103
13	The Luftwaffe In Mosul	111
14	Clearing Up: Days 16-18	116
15	Clearing Up: Days 19-31	122
16	Consequences	135
Epilogue		142
Acknowledgements		144

This sketch map shows how the Iraqi guns covered the camp at point blank range.

Map of the area, lifted from German archives (with Kingcol's 'rescue' route and English translations added).

LEGEND

∙∎∙∎∙	IRAQ BOUNDARY
—∙—∙—	OTHER NATIONAL BOUNDARIES
⌾	SWAMPS OR FLOODING
⩘	MARSHY
———	GERMAN AIRCRAFT ROUTES
—◄—	GERMAN ATTACK ROUTES
——►	BRITISH AIRCRAFT ROUTES
⊢—⊢—⊢	OIL PIPELINE
+++++	RAILWAY
▬ ▬ ▬	KINGCOL'S 'RESCUE' ROUTE

KINGCOL'S TIMETABLE

11 MAY	LEAVE NATHANYA
12 MAY	MAFRAQ
12 MAY	H.4
13/14 MAY	RUTBAH
15 MAY	KILO 50
15/16 MAY	KILO 25
17/26 MAY	HABBANIYA
27 MAY	KHAN NUQTA
30/31 MAY	BAGHDAD

MOSUL

KIRKUK

R. TIGRIS

RAILWAY

OIL PIPE LINE

RAILWAY

KHADIMAIN

HADITHA

RAILWAY

KHAN NUQTA

BA'QUBA

RAMADI

HABBANIYA

FALLUJAH

PERSIA / IRAN

BAGHDAD

KILO 25

Lake Habbaniya'

RASCHID/HINAIDI

AL MUSAYIB

FROM BASRAH

R. TIGRIS

RAQ

R. EUPHRATES

RAILWAY

BASRAH

SHAIBAH

SHATT EL ARAB

400

KUWAIT

PERSIA GULF

Preface

This book tells the story in detail of one of the most remarkable battles which took place during the Second World War. In the overall scenario, this battle was every bit as important to the war's final outcome as had been the Battle of Britain, fought seven months earlier. As in that battle, upon its outcome hung the Allies' ability to continue the war successfully. Even, in the long run maybe, to win the war at all. And, almost unbelievably, this one was fought and won against impossible odds by the unseasoned and war-inexperienced instructors of a Flying Training School, crewed by half-trained pupils.

Our near-defeat was in Iraq. And all our oil was in Iraq. The architect of the attack on us was a rabidly anti-British ex-lawyer called Raschid Ali el Gailani. At the beginning of April 1941, following a skilful coup, he became the country's self-appointed Chief of the National Defence Government. Then he set about fulfilling his ambition, which was to drive the British clear out of the Middle East by military force. To this end he enlisted the help of Egyptian hotheads who were pledged to initiate an uprising of their army, in Cairo; he also extracted a promise of help from German forces who were already in Greece. He knew that the German *Afrika Korps* was poised to drive in from the West and could count on the pro-Axis French in Syria for access to Iraq. In return, he promised the Germans unrestricted use of *all* military facilities in Iraq, British held or not.

Our High Command on the other hand, was blinded by the fact that Iraq was still politically our ally. This view, coupled with a serious misinterpretation of political and enemy intelligence, led to their belief that military force would not become a necessary factor and the final answer to problems in Iraq lay in negotiation by politicians. Indeed, the main risk they forecast was some form of riot or uprising by a rabble of the *civilian* population – until to their horror an overwhelming military force actually appeared at the perimeter of Habbaniya airfield one morning, demanding the surrender of our units there. An *armed* enemy force had never been considered or planned for by our upper levels of political and military command.

The lynch-pin to this story was a major RAF airfield, Habbaniya, sixty miles from Baghdad. It would have been vital to the Germans, both in position and in the facilities it offered, for any build-up of forces to consolidate their position in Iraq. Raschid Ali had offered it to them with unfettered use – knowing his only possible constraint was a Flying Training School based there, equipped solely with obsolescent and obsolete training aircraft. He had not, however, allowed for the fact that a small number of frustrated but fiery young instructors were breaking extensively all manner of rules and regulations dearly beloved and clung to by their elderly, nervous and out-of-date superiors. Within Habbaniya, by skipping round this restrictive 'Bull', they *doubled* the fighting potential of the school. Then in those old and fragile armed training machines, they were ready to fly and do battle.

Being 1,000 miles from the fighting war, and because of ignorance, the place was of little public interest. No public relations personnel, and no press reporters or photographers. So, for reasons brought to the surface in this carefully researched book, the story was never properly written up, pictured, or recorded at that time. Also, many major errors and failings by our higher Civil Servants and Military Commanders were carefully (and understandably) kept from public knowledge where possible. Throughout the war, and for many years after, it was played-down and referred to exclusively as 'The Iraq Rebellion' or 'The Iraq Revolt'. It has now been re-named 'The War in Iraq'. Here is the full and true story.

I beg the reader's tolerance if this story appears too egotistical. If he thinks that is so, I sincerely apologise. I was there and I have tried, with facts solely from authentic documents, and some personal opinions drawn from them, to tell of an astonishing, lonely but successful battle, beating all the odds and ending up victorious. Also, that the after-effects of that victory were of inestimable (and mainly unrecognised) value to the Allies. Full and grateful acknowledgement of my international sources is at the end.

One
Germany Ascendant: 1941

Let us first look at the Second World War situation as any intelligent Iraqi citizen could have seen it developing up to early 1941.

Germany's modern armaments had been well tried and tested in the Spanish Civil War of 1936-39. The general staff had conceived the *Blitzkrieg*, or 'Lightning-war'. They put it into practical effect by invading Poland on 1 September 1939. The overwhelming attacks and saturation bombing conquered Poland in less than four weeks.

On the Western Front there began the 'phoney war'. Nothing happened there till May 1940. The German and Allied forces did little but make faces at each other from behind the Siegfried and Maginot lines. Meanwhile, Germany used the breather we and France allowed her to good effect. She recovered her strength after the losses in Poland, and recouped her fighting potential.

Germany moved again on 9 April 1940. On that date she invaded Norway and Denmark. Denmark, mindful maybe of what had happened seven months earlier almost next door in Poland, capitulated without resistance. British and French forces landed in Norway to support resistance there.

On 10 May the Germans attacked and invaded the Netherlands, which surrendered in five days. They also broke through and overran the French line at Sedan and raced to the Channel. Thus they cut off from the French the British forces which had entered Belgium.

On 28 May King Leopold of Belgium surrendered and the tattered remnants of the British Army, together with some French troops, were evacuated from the beaches at Dunkerque over the next few days. All their arms, armour and equipment were left behind. Such of the British forces as got back to England were virtually unarmed – and we feared invasion. I clearly remember the 'Anti-Invader' weapon which my brother, also in the RAF, made for himself – his pistol having been taken from him and given to the Army. It was one third of a broomstick, with a piece of lead-pipe hammered flat and fastened round its end – as a cosh. Not much power against a Schmeisser machine-pistol, but it was the best he could do.

Italy declared war on the side of the victorious Germans on 10 June. The French signed an armistice on 22 June, permitting German occupation and control of northern France and all of its Atlantic and Channel coastline.

Germany now had control of all Denmark, the Netherlands, Belgium, and northern France, with access to the Mediterranean through Italy – all achieved in two months and thirteen days. Truly a 'Lightning-war'. Small wonder that the world saw the Germans as invincible – and the Europeans were thought useless. And this was only the beginning.

Germany intended first to drive the RAF from the skies, and break, by bombing, the British will to resist. Then, with Britain softened up, she would be nicely prepared for invasion – or capitulation like the other European countries. Barges for crossing the English Channel were prepared and gathered into the Channel ports. *'Seeloewe'* (Sealion) was the invasion's codename.

However, the Commander-in-Chief of RAF Fighter Command, Air Marshal Dowding, had clearly foreseen the certainty of the Allied military defeat by the Germans on the other side of the Channel – and its potential consequences for us. The French had squealed for RAF fighter support and Dowding had flatly refused to throw his precious fighter planes into the battle for France because sending aircraft over there would be, to use a gambler's term, 'throwing good money after bad'.

He may well have been influenced also by his knowledge of the stocks of French fighter-aircraft. They held, in reserve in the south-west of France, at the time of their cries for our support, more fighters than were in the whole of RAF Fighter Command. They were not the latest types, but worth calling into battle as a last resort; the French did no such thing. Dowding husbanded his Hurricanes and Spitfires for the big battle with the Germans which he was sure would come. This master-stroke enraged many of our politicians and the French, who were more self-interested and less perspicacious than Dowding. His refusal to bow to political pressure was one of the keys to our ultimate victory. It earned him conspicuous unpopularity at that time but, in history, undying fame. In July of 1940, the big battle came – the Battle of Britain – and the air-combats were tremendous.

For a long time, several German generals considered that the only viable strategy for beating Britain was to make all-out air-attacks on some major cities. *Feldmarschall* Albert Kesselring was a major protagonist of this theory. He believed it would cause such extreme damage and casualties that it would break our will to resist – it had worked in Spain, Poland and Holland, so why not Britain?

It was the Germans themselves who triggered their ultimate failure, by mistake. On 25 August a lost and lonely German bomber dropped a few bombs on London. Bomber Command promptly responded by dropping some bombs on Berlin. Hitler was furious. He had loudly proclaimed to his people that it could never occur. He demanded retribution. The point was not lost on Kesselring who now had an opportunity to voice his contentions more strongly than ever. Perhaps it was because of this pressure that *Reichsmarschall* Hermann Göring, Head of the German Luftwaffe, obtained Adolf Hitler's permission to change tactics. This was a crass error, breaking one of the principles of war – Maintenance of the Aim. He thereby unwittingly came to our rescue. Göring stopped attacking our fighter defence *before* it had been broken, as it might well have been if he had continued.

At the end of August, contrary to official reports published at the time, Fighter Command was indeed very near the knuckle. It is almost certain that victory was on the point of being snatched from our remaining, exhausted, fighter-team. But, whatever his reasons for not going all out to drive our Hurricanes and Spitfires from the skies, on 7 September Göring switched his German fighters to escorting and defending the bombers as they attacked our ports and the cities, by day and by night. Göring's change of tactic gave Fighter Command the respite which it so desperately needed. At the end of September, after three months of heavy fighting, the RAF most unreasonably continued its refusal to be driven from the combat. Control of the air, vital for any invasion from the continent of Europe, had not been achieved. Sealion was first of all delayed, and then finally cancelled by the end of the year. This acceptance by Germany of failure – defeat if you will – in the Battle of Britain was the only misstep in her progress so far – and even that was not obvious to an outsider.

Also, luckily for us, Göring's switch to attacking towns fared no better in softening up our country for an enforced or negotiated peace.

Nobody, even in Britain, realised quite what had happened – until the change in Göring's tactics was fully perceived. No one, particularly the RAF pilots involved, knew that their 'failure to lose' the air-battle they had been fighting would turn out to be 'a major victory' – a victory crucial to the whole war. No defeat or victory was publicised, or even seen to have occurred, until that great Prime Minister of Britain, Winston Churchill, uttered the famous words, 'Never in the field of human conflict has so much been owed by so many to so few.' Only then did victory in the Battle of Britain become apparent.

There was, as well, an unnoticed result which was to take on deep significance later. It was not fully appreciated at the time in Britain; it assuredly became painfully apparent to the German High Command as the war progressed. Failure to eliminate Britain had inevitably forced Germany into a long war – and she did not have the oil stocks nor the oil-production capacity to sustain a protracted conflict. She needed oil desperately – lots of it. Failure to reach oil supplies, in Russia or elsewhere, was to become another nail in Germany's wartime coffin. In Russia, and also in Europe after the Allied invasion of 1944, lack of oil was a prime factor in her ultimate defeat.

In 1940 Italy entered the Balkans with the intention of capturing Greece, but they were promptly pushed back as far as Albania. The Germans followed them and, by the end of the year, they were far into the Balkans, advancing on Greece and doing well.

In North Africa, during the autumn of 1940 the Italian Army and Air Force tried again. They attacked the British forces based in Egypt, from their bases in Tripolitania, Libya, and Cyrenaica. By December they were roundly and soundly trounced for their pains by General Wavell's army and a small supporting force of the RAF. The Italian forces in Africa were effectively neutralised and 200,000 prisoners of war were taken.

It was not all bad news for all Italians. I had collected two prisoners for the domestic staff of my tented Officers' Mess in the Western Desert. They were delighted not to be in prison, were first-class cooks, and highly co-operative.

One morning at dawn a German Heinkel 111 bomber flew low overhead. I was startled to hear a stream of machine-gun fire and to see tracer-bullets rising up to it, for we had no ground-defence. It proved to be our two cooks, who had 'liberated' and prepared a captured Italian gun with its ammunition. They could have taken my entire squadron hostage! However, they explained earnestly that they had no intention of fighting again, on anybody's side, and were fully determined to preserve their new-found freedom against all comers – Germans and Italians included. Admittedly, our enemy in possession of the only ground-gun in the place was somewhat disquieting, but I forgave them. Our ex-enemy cooks continued happily as my operational ground-defence unit – until someone decreed that they should go to a prisoner-of-war camp, and took them away.

Wavell's forces advanced 500 miles right up to Benghazi and should have gone much further, but for three elements. First, our lines of supply were terribly extended. Secondly, the British High Command gave instructions for substantial slices of his forces – both Army and RAF – to be sent to Greece to try and stem the German advance southwards in that country. Thirdly, German forces – the famous *Afrika Korps* under *Feldmarshall* Rommel and supported by the Luftwaffe – were pouring into North Africa, to begin their sporadic advance eastwards. Almost every man in the *Afrika Korps* was well aware that the ultimate objective Rommel had set himself was Iraqi oil. The word 'sporadic' is used deliberately because, despite early successes against Wavell's thinned-out forces, it was not all a one-way affair. It was much later, after some brilliance and some luck, that Rommel acquired his myth of invincibility. The British forces remaining in the desert caused Rommel a lot of to-ing and fro-ing, back and forth, along the North African coastline. Which is how the British Army and the RAF acquired the derogatory nickname 'Benghazi Harriers'. A halt to his progress was achieved in July 1942, near a coastal fishing village called El Alamein. It was only about 50 miles from our naval base of Alexandria. The victory of Alamein is in itself is a fascinating story which, however, is not for telling here.

In early 1941, in Whitehall, by far the greatest threats for the Allies appeared to be from the Balkans, Greece, the Western Desert and Crete – with sinister overtones in Cyprus, Syria and Turkey. Headquarters Middle East felt the same. They reacted more readily and positively to reports on those areas, and only half-heartedly to those dealing with lesser spots – such as Iraq.

The Iraqis, of course, were well aware by early 1941 that any initiative appeared to continue wholly in German hands. Consider their successes! Poland, Norway, Denmark, Belgium, Holland, France, Italy, the Balkans, Greece – and North Africa well towards the Nile Delta – all under German control. The result of the Battle of Britain was negative; nothing much looked to have changed. To outsiders, Britain was an island, cut off and likely to be starved into surrender by German submarines, particularly as America was still strongly isolationist and keeping firmly out of harm's way.

If any country were considering a best line of action and throwing in its lot with either the Allies or the Axis, personal advantage and prudence would surely dictate the choice of Germany and her partner, Italy. Even to a neutral (and the Iraqis were far from neutral) nowhere could Germany be seen a loser. On the contrary, everywhere she was clearly and obviously in the ascendant, and apparently invincible.

The Iraqis may have been our allies politically, but many of them – especially those holding the reins of power – hated our guts.

Two
The Crisis and The Historians

The Crisis

The Battle of Britain in 1940 and its critical importance to the outcome of the Second World War is widely known and remembered annually on a national basis. The daily average fighting strength of pilots in the battle (depending on which book you read) was somewhere between 700 and 1,400. About 2,500 aircrew (pilots and others) qualified for the Battle of Britain medal. Most of them came from RAF Fighter Command.

Between the beginning of April and the beginning of May 1941, a series of connected high-level, monumental cock-ups brought us right to the brink of a military disaster which this book brings to light. That disaster was avoided by a feat of arms that went virtually unrecognised at the time and for many years thereafter.

Seven months after the Battle of Britain, an air battle of equally vital importance for the outcome of the war took place. It was in Iraq, the source of all our oil. The pilots who fought and won the brief and bloody Battle of Habbaniya came from No. 4 Flying Training School. The majority of the thirty-nine pilots were unseasoned flying instructors. They had out-of-date and hastily armed training planes and a total lack of supporting ground-based facilities. Any supporting aircrew they did have, had been drawn from among sixty of the pupils, who were press-ganged for any and every task. Hopelessly outclassed and outnumbered, the team flung itself against a besieging modern Iraqi Army, supported by their modern Air Force. The casualties in men and machines were devastating. There were only thirty-nine pilots to start with, and a quarter of those few pilots were lost in the first *fourteen hours*. Four more pilots joined them on the third day.

After five days and four nights of a horrendous twenty-four-hour-a-day air-attack the well-equipped Iraqi Army was completely demoralised. It fled, routed, never to reappear and fight. Next, strengthened by some reinforcement aircraft and crews flown in from elsewhere, the School also mopped up the Iraqi Air Force. A week later, the German Luftwaffe arrived in Iraq, as expected by the Iraqi Command, to take a hand. Its brief was to help the Iraqi armed forces capture RAF Habbaniya. But it was too little and too late. Thanks to the Flying Training School, the Iraqi Army declined to fight. The school, reinforced, duly mopped the Germans up as well. Complete victory took a month in all.

In May 1941, if the decision had not been made to send the School into battle in spite of all its inadequacies, and if those forty-three pilots had not then won the ensuing fight, we almost certainly would have lost Iraq – with all our oil. That success for the enemy would have nipped out our vital power-base in Egypt. The essential build-up of air and ground forces in the Nile-Delta, for General Montgomery's victory at Alamein fifteen months later, could never have been made. All that the 2,500 Battle of Britain aircrew had gained from their air-war seven months earlier would have been lost. But it was not lost and our success at Alamein proved to be *the* crucial turning point that opened the way to win the war in the Middle East and in Europe.

Just forty-three pilots and some pupils won the battle. It sounds unlikely, but it happens to be true. Churchill and other historians paid the School its due, much later on – and in more measured and statesman-like terms than mine.

The Historians

I am filling in for the future a piece of little-known history. For a variety of reasons, many of the written records of the events to be described are either wrong or at best distorted. Others are undoubtedly true. Which can really be dismissed as fiction? Which are fact? Fact and fiction have, inevitably, been intermingled; but I believe that here I have retained hardly any fiction, and very few errors of fact. First, I have had recent access to material which was unavailable to British authors of the official records – such as that in the German Luftwaffe archives. Second, and best of all, in peacetime I have had time to think and compare sources. All of it is as near to fact as I have been able to achieve. Additionally I sincerely hope that I have made it easier to read than all that dry official stuff.

I want this to stand for all time as not only the most accurate but also the most reliable record to be found of an astonishing, unlikely and unique war-success.

The story is drawn from official records and Service documents both British and foreign, from press articles based on those records, from books by authors using notes made during the campaign itself, from letters written by people who were there, and from a narrative report checked and authenticated by Air Headquarters Iraq before being placed with the official RAF records. I have collected stories and letters from all the people I could trace and contact. But, too few of the young men who surrounded me are alive and available to record their similar stories, and they are lost forever. None of these many sources, alone, gives a complete account. Further, each and every one contains some mistakes. However, every significant event in this book is factual and documented somewhere. Partly from interest, and partly in justification of my comments, it is worth demonstrating some differences.

To some extent the precise history of events in RAF Habbaniya during the months of April and May 1941, is and always will be, obscured by mists of ambiguity and be open to argument here and there. The reasons are simple; imperfections in the remaining records come both from normal faults in human nature, and from bad luck.

For example, there were no reporters, no photographers, no public-relations people making notes and taking pictures which could be used to jog memories. Also, memory alone is fallible. In my research, different people who were on the spot have recalled clearly to me quite different memories of the same event, and nothing would shake their personal conviction that their own version was the accurate one.

Fortunately, any divergence from the truth was minor, and cannot affect the main story with its undisputed outcome. Let us look at a few of the errors.

Many faults in the recorded history of the Iraq War spring from the departure of the main boss at the outset and a space of nearly three weeks before his successor arrived. During that time, all hell was let loose. Inevitably, the middle-bracket bodies like myself, working ourselves to utter exhaustion, tended to be intensely and mainly preoccupied with the howling conflict raging about us. We took little time, if any, to make written records of anything at all which posterity might see.

Another type of error comes from the 'Not My Business' syndrome. There was a group captain, Commander of the School, who kept himself almost exclusively incarcerated in his office, working wonders at administration. Our supply of bombs, ammunition, fuel and oil never faltered. Indeed, his records of the total sorties flown by his School's aircraft, as he saw them, are precise and accurate. Likewise he noted carefully the numbers of men from his School who were killed or wounded. But, he had a tidy mind. We, his juniors, had hijacked other men from every possible source to help us; these were not *his* men and he did not see a need to record casualties from among the visitors – because they did not officially belong to his own unit. A peculiar point of view for there was no one elsewhere in a position to make those recordings – so our heavy casualties were, in fact, officially *understated*.

Take one example: Air Marshal Sir Paul Holder, a pilot, was then a wing commander whom we co-opted from a staff-post in Station Headquarters to fly a school aircraft. He tells me that he was shot down twice, but survived – and he, of all people, should know the truth beyond doubt. Yet, neither of his crashes appears in the group captain's archives. For similar reasons, we pilots were flying flat-out, often darting off on a second sortie without reporting formally to the group captain or recording every sortie made. Consequently, his figures (the official ones) for different targets struck and numbers of aircraft on each, with results achieved, are short of the truth.

To compound matters, almost every military leader delegates to some minion below him the chore of writing his Operations Record Book. From this, and other papers, the Official History will be compiled, eventually. Elsewhere, I have myself delegated that task. Inevitably the unenvied job gets gradually shuffled down the ladder of seniority until it bottoms out, for example, on some unlucky Flying Officer in the Intelligence Branch, or perhaps an Assistant Adjutant. This poor soul is bluntly told to get on with it, as good training for him. He has neither the rank nor the clout to pass the buck back up again, or find someone below to whom he can pass it on.

The hapless embryo-author is then left, sometimes many months or even years later, to do the best he can from whatever fragmentary records there are to be unearthed, slowly and by degrees. As like as not, this unfortunate may easily have never written a piece since school, nor been near the scene while it was all going on; half of those who were there have left – the other half are too occupied even to give him sympathy, let alone help. Or, as in this case, they may be dead.

The Air Historical Branch of the RAF recalls its most blatant example of irrevocable loss from forced authorship. Two years of history for a flying squadron (including a Royal Visit) had been abbreviated by the recording officer to one single sheet of paper. And everything else of interest for that squadron during two years was lost forever.

At Habbaniya, Air Vice-Marshal John D'Albiac was the replacement boss arriving from Greece as the campaign was drawing to its close. He was not there for the battle, and had no first-hand knowledge of it. However, the official history of the battle, as written later on, stands forever as his – and so it must; he was the officer who signed it. It is not surprising that, with the best will in the world, of the many matters of battle detail at Habbaniya, some were never committed to any form of paper at that time; some facts and figures are missing; some were recorded only in general terms; and some are, quite simply, wrong. Two mistakes only, taken from D'Albiac's official historical record, will be enough to illustrate my point.

His official history says that the battle began with thirty Audax aircraft, in three squadrons of ten. This is nearly true, but not quite. Thirty Audaxes, were there – yes – but a different piece of paper elsewhere notes, more accurately, that the School could only find the bomb-racks and guns for twenty-one, so only that number could join the fight. The battle actually opened with only two squadrons of Audaxes, nine and twelve, totalling twenty-one.

It also records that there were two Iraqi bombing raids on 6 May 1941, but that no casualties were suffered. *No* casualties suffered? Tucked away is another statement alleging that, among other losses, there were five men killed and four wounded. Which is correct? I can state irrefutably that D'Albiac's official history, sadly, is false. Sergeant Prickett, my bomb-aimer, my friend and my team-mate of many raids, was outside loading our machine with more bombs when a raid occurred – because we saved time by taking it in turns to report to the group captain's office. Hearing the roar of Iraqi aircraft and the crash of explosive I ran out and knelt beside my fallen colleague. I felt for his heartbeat. He was dead.

None of the errors I have mentioned has any significant bearing on the ultimate and actual result of our fight, and to my mind they can all be set aside as immaterial. I like to feel confident, however, that my book is a document substantially more accurate than the official record subsequently ghosted for Air Marshal D'Albiac. He would probably have agreed with me; he was not the type of man who would claim reliable accuracy for his signed story of a period when he wasn't there, wasn't in control, didn't write it and who was denied the inestimable value of hindsight.

I have tried, with facts drawn solely from authentic documents, and some personal opinions drawn from them, to demonstrate that the School fought an astonishing, lonely but successful battle, ending up victorious. Also, that the after-effects of that victory were of inestimable yet generally unrecognised value to the Allies.

If you think this tale appears to be unreasonably egotistic, that is not my purpose. If you, the reader thinks that is so, I sincerely apologise. Shrug my views off if you will. But, I was there at the time and I wish to tell a more truthful and complete story than can be found anywhere else. I took a significant part in the proceedings and that is of some value to the whole.

There is an old Chinese saying – 'The Many-Sidedness of Truth', individual pieces of my complete story, with which different readers disagree, might be dismissed as just that.

My tale starts when Iraq was an outpost of the British Empire, in the 1920s.

Three
Gunboat Diplomats

Between 1920 and 1930, after the Great War to end all wars, Iraq was effectively part of that British Empire upon which the sun never set. We kept the peace. It was a Third World country and peace was normally disturbed only when the local tribes and the more malleable sections of the indigenous population rose in defiance of authority. For theologians and historians who study the influence of religious leaders, the situation in the Middle East then was much as it is now in many parts of the world. The prime stirrers-up of such trouble were the teachers of religion and the law – in the Islamic case, the Muftis and the Mullahs. Our method of restoring order perhaps smacked of 'Gunboat Diplomacy', but it was both effective among the tribesmen and caused no loss of life after having been refined for a few years.

Peace was kept in a way devised by the father of the Air Force, the late Lord Trenchard. His first trial run was in Somaliland. There, the troublesome pot-stirrer in about 1920 was a Mullah, known as the Mad Mullah. His followers judged that fighting on the ground gave the prospect of hijacking some booty, and probably gathering in a few rifles. It was value for effort! One day the Mad Mullah triggered off an uprising and the British Army made plans to handle it. It costed out in the terms of two divisions of troops to suppress the Mullah and his supporters. Trenchard offered to complete the task with two RAF squadrons.

He was right. That was all it took and, at the time, was hailed as the cheapest war ever known. Regrettably, being a first experiment, his operations were far too brutal. The Mad Mullah was killed and the revolt was quelled in a matter of days. However, it showed that the use of aircraft, against which the rebels had no counter, could be remarkably cheap and extremely demoralising for the insurgents.

The use of aircraft by the British soon became much more gentlemanly. Force, in terms of bombs and machine-gunning was there but it was kept in reserve, a threat, to be used in default of good behaviour. Like the splendid old-fashioned local policeman who kept order among the youths in his own streets, 'Behave yourself my lads, or if you don't, I'll give you a good hearty clip over the ear!' it was blunt, quick and effective.

In the very early days of flying over the Third World, the local population was simple and generally uneducated. First, and always at the behest of the political masters, pamphlets would be dropped, couched in unequivocal terms, saying that if the trouble did not cease forthwith, penalties would be inflicted and fines levied on whatever scale the politicians had decided. Failing peace, aircraft would be sent to patrol their fields and crops. There, from above the range of the farmers' ancient muskets, they would watch to ensure that no farming could be done. Agriculture, essential for their normal livelihood, would be suspended. If any tried to contravene those orders and till their lands, then (and only then) might they be attacked from the air. In the most extreme cases, again after ample warning for protection of life, houses or a village might be knocked down by bombing. Aircraft had become a political and economic tool, available on demand by the local government. Persuasion came from touching the pockets and not the persons of the miscreants – the warlike farmers. But they knew clearly that the sword was available, always, even if normally kept sheathed in the background. It was not an empty threat and, ninety-nine times out of a hundred, the sight of our aircraft overhead was enough to bring the hotheads to bargaining point.

This one-sided bargain was enforceable because those to be controlled were uneducated and only the British wielded the big stick – aeroplanes. It meant that the farmers could be placed under financial duress without any loss of life. An early form of sanctions. It worked splendidly for many years between the wars wherever political control over a peasant-farmer population was requested from the RAF. On the whole, British influence was certainly more beneficial than harmful.

This, for three years between 1936 and '38 had been my RAF job, in the north-western corner of the Indian sub-continent. I helped to keep the peace among wily and warring Pathan tribes up in the mountains near the border with Afghanistan. Naturally, I undertook a variety of other tasks as well, from photographic-survey to flying a sick soldier to hospital. But, peacekeeping was the burden of my work. I learned a lot about the techniques, the necessity for self-reliance and accurate pilot-navigation (for we had no radio or navigator) and also with some alarm I learned what horrible injury the local populace (or, more accurately, their womenfolk) might inflict upon your 'family jewels' if you happened to be brought down among them.

In 1930, Britain and Iraq despite all the adverse myths before, at the time and since, voluntarily came to an agreement and signed an Anglo-Iraq Treaty of Alliance and Mutual Support. It was an affirmation of continuing friendship established and carefully spelled out in the document, with its annexes.

On one side, by this Treaty, Britain fully recognised the independence and sovereignty of Iraq, its King and its Government. On the other side, in return for receiving the reins of internal politics and the peacekeeping role that went with it, the Iraqis would permit the British to station troops and aircraft in the country at two bases, to be held on leases for as long as the Treaty existed. Permission was freely given by the Iraqis. Agreement was included that Britain would co-operate closely with Iraq for many reasons, advantageous to both nations. Nothing very sophisticated was envisaged. We undertook to try and prevent marauders starting to make trouble in the first place, by using our aircraft in the traditional peacekeeping role. At the same time, our installations would have to have troops and arms to make the threats effective. Also, we would have armament stocks for dropping bombs or using machine-guns if the tribesmen became too restive. On their side, they would protect British interests after the take-over of political power. Moreover, if trouble broke out, they undertook to guard and protect our installations from attack by tribesmen or any other armed forces. If there was any menace of forces entering the country from outside, both nations would co-operate in mutual defence.

The two bases which the RAF occupied, Hinaidi[1] and Mosul, would remain in our hands for five years after the Treaty was signed. Hinaidi, our main base, was just outside the capital city Baghdad. Mosul was 240 miles to the north. The understanding was that our local headquarters and the squadrons would in due course move out to other airfields. The main force location, still to be selected, would lie somewhere between Baghdad and the Syrian border. Five years was allowed for the project, because everything would have to be created entirely from scratch. The other base would be moved to an airfield on the edge of the Persian Gulf, near the town of Basrah. It would bear the name of a local village, Shaibah, but to simplify and avoid confusion in this story, one name only – Basrah – has been used for both town and airfield. They were only a few miles apart.

Lastly, to support our military and trade interests in both directions, from Egypt on the one side to India and beyond on the other, free passage for our troops backwards and forwards was also written into the Treaty.

In sum, our presence there was for peacekeeping, and protection of trade mainly in the form of our oil-supplies. The Iraqis agreed to help us in that aim to the best of their ability. All in all, what with ceding power to the Iraqis, the work that would be created and the money for them which would come into the country, it seemed that a pleasant mutual co-operation and admiration society had been created.

In addition to our two permanent bases we had several landing-grounds from which detachments could operate. Facilities would today seem unbelievably primitive and surroundings have changed out of all recognition. Take for example, a small island half way along the Persian Gulf on the side facing Persia, now called Iran. Behind it, on the mainland, lay a small town; perhaps 'large village' would be a better description. On the island was a dried up salt-flat which was the local landing-ground, because, if no rain had fallen and luckily it very seldom did, it was quite hard enough for the early biplanes to land on. I landed there myself in 1937, in just such a machine. From the town you reached the island by rowing boat. There was talk of building a causeway, to ride a donkey across, but no work was going on and 'no see – no believe!' There was one small wooden hut, with no occupants. Its key was kept at the police station in the 'large village' over on the mainland. Having got the key I brewed a mug of tea which I drank, sitting on the floor with my back against the wall under the veranda, sweating profusely. Before me the local Arabs casually drove their herds of sheep, and camels carrying goods for trade, around my aeroplane and across the landing-ground. The windsock looked very unattended as it swung lazily from the top of a slim pole which had once been a length of galvanised-iron water-pipe.

That bare and simple salt-pan has grown into the vast complex of terminal buildings, hotels, restaurants, air conditioning, radio-masts, searchlights, beacons, roads, aircraft

[1]Hinaidi was the Iraqi Air Force Headquarters

parking-areas, taxi-tracks and runways that is now Bahrain International Airport. A causeway has been built, across which you may drive a car to and from the mainland, and most of the local Arabs appear to have exchanged camels and donkeys for Cadillacs. Such is progress.

Bear in mind, however, that all the time that Bahrain was being modernised in the Persian Gulf, Iraq itself and its people were also developing equally remarkably. Iraq had always been a turbulent country. Oceans of oil were found and money came pouring in. Schools became commonplace. Education advanced. This mental and economic growth of the Iraqi population was not fully appreciated by us and dangerously unrecognised in many of our high places. As time passed, it was of course inevitable that all the nationalistic factions in Iraq and elsewhere should seek to break loose from our so-called Imperialistic bonds. Our top brass and top politicians did not realise (or want to believe?) that the sight of a few British aeroplanes flying around would soon no longer be enough to make the majority of the people below come running to parley, upon *our* terms!

In 1931, the site for the new RAF base was selected. It would be astride the trans-desert road from the Mediterranean to the Iraqi capital, immediately alongside the Euphrates river – some 60 miles from Baghdad and 200 miles from Rutbah Wells. Rutbah was the site of an old-fashioned fort and a new-fashioned pumping plant sending oil to the west. It had a small landing ground beside the pipeline and was fairly near the Syrian border on the way to Damascus, Jordan and beyond.

A couple of miles to the south of the base itself, on the opposite side to the river, and behind a 200ft escarpment which overlooked the camp, was a sizeable freshwater lake, Lake Habbaniya. This would be an alighting point and refuelling point for the Imperial Airways flying boats, on their journeys to and from the lands of our British Empire.

The new airfield-complex took about five years to build and it was a marvellous operation. Tucked into bends of the River Euphrates, it was a vast undertaking for its era. Even the domestic accommodation for the locally-enlisted staff and guards covered about 500 acres. Hangars, workshops, offices, telephone exchange, living quarters, messes, sports facilities – anything in fact which needed to be protected from light-fingered pilferers – was safely protected inside the six-mile long fence. Also in there were the filtration plant and a power station for electric supply; the precaution of duplicating these vital services was not however taken. Were they not in a friendly country? There were no dispersal areas, no bomb-proof shelters, no redoubts and no safe hidey-holes. If it ever became a target, it would be a very 'soft' one.

On the side furthest from the river was a sizeable airfield. Puny maybe, if compared to a modern airport like Heathrow or Gatwick with their 3,000-yard runways, but substantial for 1935. It gave landing runs of 1,000 yards in two directions. The airfield was not inside the perimeter fence because it was thought to be unnecessary – and too expensive – to protect an airfield of packed sand on the edge of a sandy desert in an allied country.

The really impressive elements, however, were the off-duty amenities. There were playing fields for rugger, soccer, and hockey. There was a golf course. Riding stables held the ponies for hacking, or playing polo on the polo-pitch. Both polo-pitch and golf course were beside each other, right in the middle of the camp. The lake, just up and over the escarpment on the other side of the airfield, could be used by the local RAF Yacht Club and for open-water bathing. Within the camp, there was also the finest swimming pool in the Service. The gymnasium was superb and there were fifty-six tennis courts.

Being on the very bank of the River Euphrates there was ample water for irrigation. The place did its best to be something of a garden. Lawns and flower beds were everywhere. Bougainvillaea plants climbed up and blossomed over the walls of messes and sleeping-quarters. Fast-growing eucalyptus, pepper and casuarina trees lined its twenty-eight miles of roads. Even the roads were reminiscent of home, being named after such British landmarks as the Strand, Piccadilly, and Regent Street. Others carried the names of famous RAF personalities from bygone years – Sefton-Branker, Salmond, Ball and many more.

Everything had been done to make the place a pleasant oasis in a barren and inhospitable desert. Well, nearly everything.

Before the Second World War our Government, ostensibly in the interests of Service Efficiency but doubtless also prompted by Treasury economy, did not recognise any right or need of a young and therefore junior live-wire in the Air Force to support a wife. No married accommodation would be provided until the Services had given permission – and without that permission no marriage allowances might be paid in order to help with accommodation off the base. Women were officially ignored and any kind of liaison on the distaff side was actively discouraged until a man was thirty years old or held the rank of Squadron Leader – but in those days of slow promotion hardly anybody reached Squadron Leader before the age of thirty anyway.

Abroad, the practice was compounded by the doctors. They gave official credence to a myth that women were incapable of sustaining the heat of the desert and at the same time retaining their health. Air conditioning was no answer, either because it had not been invented or was too expensive for the Treasury to contemplate. There were no cool mountain-tops, as in India, to which the womenfolk might be sent to escape the 'hot-weather'. Either way, Iraq was classed as a 'Two-Year Unaccompanied' area; partly because there was no private accommodation anyway (even for one of the extremely rare wealthy servicemen who had enough money to pay for it). And, partly from the standard RAF regulations backed up by the medical fraternity allegedly to preserve the health of those fragile creatures – women. Ordinarily, none were allowed there. Full stop. And any man posted there pre-war, married or not, faced a two-year stint in the place, on his own. The dearth of female company was uncomfortable, to say the least.

No sweeping statement is ever wholly true. There were two exceptions to this 'no women' rule. First, the Air Officer Commanding could and did have his wife and daughter with him, lucky fellow. Secondly, in the hospital there were a few nurses, thank goodness. Contrary to what the doctors said about other women, the AOC's family and those angels of mercy remained apparently healthy, vigorous and happy. There were all too few of them, but it made a marvellous difference to see them around. And, if you were one of the select few officers by whom they might choose to be squired from time to time, life was immeasurably good. Jealousy for one's own position, particularly when displayed by colleagues, is marvellously flattering to a man. Officers maybe, but the airmen had no such female contact.

A wartime duty I detested was censoring personal mail, to ensure there were no breaches of security. I hated being privy to my men's most private thoughts and did my utmost to retain total anonymity. Occasionally, under the awful strain of no female company they so starkly bared their very souls that it almost hurt me to know it. One man wrote to his wife, 'Darling; for God's sake have the bedroom ceiling painted a colour you like, because it's all you're going to see for a couple of months after I get back.' Another was writing to his girlfriend. He penned a long and friendly letter and ended it as so many did with the classic old-fashioned phrase: 'Hoping this finds you as it leaves me, in the pink. Your loving, Charlie.' Then, noting it was a girlfriend and he was not even engaged to her, I thought he rather lowered the tone by adding at the end: 'PS I'm not half going to **** you when I get home.' I broke my rule to be blind except for a breach of security. I sent back a note from 'the censor'. I suggested that as his letter was so personal and would doubtless be greatly valued by his friend, it might be more tactful to put his feelings in the body of the missive, and not merely appended as an apparent afterthought.

In 1937 the RAF Air Headquarters moved from Hinaidi to the new base (called RAF Dhibban at that time) together with a couple of RAF Squadrons for continued peacekeeping among the unruly Kurdish farmer-tribesmen. The base at Mosul was given to the Iraqis and its RAF population was moved to Basrah.

In retrospect, it is interesting to learn why no preparation was made for an attack upon Habbaniya (our main base) by a determined enemy, who that enemy might be, nor what might be done if it happened.

On 28 July 1933, just before building began, the matter was raised in Whitehall because Lord Hailsham was apprehensive about 'the difficulty and dangers of extricating the Royal Air Force in the event of trouble in Iraq.' The italics below are mine, and the content of the sentences are worth bearing in mind when reading what happened later:

First, Lord Hailsham was answered by a letter from Lord Londonderry in October. It stated that as long as the Anglo-Iraq Treaty was in effect,

> *...no hostile act by the Iraqi Government against our forces could reasonably be contemplated.*

Second, the defence of Habbaniya was assessed to be of little consequence because our forces were adequately safeguarded by the existence of the Treaty

> *...except perhaps against recalcitrant tribesmen who, it was reasonable to assume, would be suppressed by the Iraqi Government.... Therefore, only tribesmen could pose a risk, and the Iraqi Government would deal with the matter...because they were pledged by Treaty to come to our aid if needs be.*

Following through and making deductions about the thinking of our planners in 1933 is a real eye-opener. No aircraft at that time had the range to reach it from outside Iraq for an attack; so they took the view that Habbaniya was too far from any potential front line in any foreseeable war for an outside enemy to pose a significant threat. Thus, the wishful thinking of the local planners, in line with that of their political masters, came down to only one apparent danger – local rioters. As the camp was sixty miles from the nearest town they assumed that only a meagre number of rioters could get there in order to congregate on the airfield before the Treaty-bound and pro-British Iraqi Government would disperse the crowds themselves.

Whatever the precise details of their thinking may have been, virtual peacetime conditions for the indefinite future in Habbaniya seem to have been assumed. In the high places that thinking persisted. It remained right up to and into the second year of the Second World War. It proved in practice to be fundamentally flawed. The excitable country, Iraq, should not have been trusted to remain content with the Treaty and be a sound guardian of our installations – as they had promised and as we continued to assume. Shortly after the outbreak of Hitler's war in 1939, the operational squadrons had their old-fashioned biplanes removed. They were re-equipped with more modern monoplanes and sent off to do battle for King and Country in the vicinity of Egypt. As a safety precaution, No. 4 Flying Training School was uprooted from Ismailia alongside the Suez Canal and transferred to the new and renamed complex – far, far from the shooting-war. Air Headquarters Iraq, based at Habbaniya, settled down to its prime task, aircrew training – presumably 'for the duration'.

Throughout this story a mass of curious or poor strategic decisions in Iraq by the British – as well as some by our enemies – will come to light. This, however, does not prove that our Service commanders were inexcusably incompetent. Admittedly, immediate responsibility for decisions in good time (or lack of them) lies with Commanders at all levels but, give them their due, they can only make decisions on their analysis and understanding of the information they receive. Conflicting pressures and demands on all our forces throughout the Middle East were enormous. The wider assessment of our Middle East problems was given to the local Commanders-in-Chief to undertake by Whitehall. Topmost brass certainly misjudged the Iraqis, believing them to have remained more illiterate, ignorant and scared of aircraft than was in fact the case. Undue weight was given to a view that they were our allies so, with some exceptions, basically they were believed to be on our side. Whatever may have been the truth as to the thinking at that point in time, we can now see many errors of judgement. Some are barely believable. Nevertheless, all the time, all the way down the chain, various extenuating factors should be sought, for the easy-come wisdom of hindsight is satisfying only to the man who is looking backwards over the shoulders of other, and usually better, men.

Four
Iraq: 1920 to 1941

One would think that in twenty-one years the general tenor and sentiments within Iraq would change. By 1941 might it not have settled down perhaps? Don't you believe it! The most cursory glance at the history of troubles in the country shows that there was virtually no change in the general pattern of mutual and local strife, before or after, with or without our Treaty added in 1930. The only visible change was that on the whole the Iraqis gradually took over their own housekeeping instead of having it done for them by us.

In the 1920s, a certain Sheikh Mahmoud made many attempts to gain control of Kurdistan, up in the north of Iraq. Between 1924 and 1927 there were disturbances at intervals, they would come and go, in several parts of the country. These resulted in intermittent air-operations by us. Sundry villages were bombed without loss of life, after the usual warnings. Peace, more-or-less, held.

In 1927, Sheikh Mahmoud was joined by another Sheikh, Ahmed of Barzan. This time there was intensive air action in conjunction with a force of Iraqi levies and the situation was restored. In 1930 Sheikh Mahmoud made his final determined attempt to set himself up in Kurdistan as head of a Kurdish state. Once more the RAF co-operated, this time with the Iraq Army. The Sheikh surrendered and was flown by the RAF to internal exile at Ur. The Treaty of 1930 came into existence and thereafter the Iraqi Government was effectively on its own. In 1932 the Iraqi Government tried to assert its authority, virtually by itself, over the Kurds. It was a dismal failure, and the RAF was compelled to take over the whole operation for them. As a result of our help the Iraqi Government was able to establish a civil administration throughout the area.

In 1933, King Faisal, a long-standing friend of the British, died and was succeeded by his son, Ghazi, aged twenty-one. Almost immediately after his accession there was trouble among the Iraqi Assyrian population. It was ruthlessly and brutally suppressed by the Iraqis. This was very embarrassing for us because we employed Assyrian Levies on local defence and guard duties, and naturally they learned of the horrific punishments meted out by their Government upon their blood-brothers. What troubled them even more was that we did not step in to impose our usual restraint. Their loyalty to us was deeply strained although, in the end, they remained with us and for us. However, from that moment the Iraqi Assyrians, deep down, though continuing their aversion to our presence as a matter of principle, detested their Iraqi national rulers far more than they resented us.

Next, it was the Rani Huchaim tribal confederation which erupted. They too were ruthlessly suppressed by the Iraqi Air Force and Army. Then Barzan came up again, joining forces with the Qurna area and the Yezidi tribe. By 1935 the 'normal' and periodic uprisings were all being controlled or one might say, more accurately, 'forcefully put down' by the Iraqi Government and they did not seek our help. These uprisings were all far from our bases; we did not need to become involved and we chose to do nothing.

In 1936 there was a military *coup d'état* , which resulted in the formation of a Nationalist Government. Although the Nationalists tended to be anti-British, they nevertheless expressed outwardly a firm intention to conform to our 1930 Treaty. Therefore, as far as the British chose to believe, nothing seemed to have changed a great deal.

We persuaded ourselves (wishful thinking maybe?) that the Anglo-Iraqi Treaty was working splendidly and we adopted a position of masterly inactivity. In retrospect this inactivity was very unwise. All this time, Arab Nationalism had been increasing in all countries of the Middle East, and Iraq was no exception. The British presence through the years, whether beneficent or not, became more and more resented.

The anti-British feeling had not been lost upon Germany. By this time, the Germans had become deeply involved in sowing seeds of unrest in Iraq's fertile hot-house.

Their intrigues had been in progress since 1933. German influence had been skilfully expanded under the direction and guidance of a highly efficient Envoy at their Legation, *Doktor* Grobba. His fingers were in every pie – commercial, cultural, and political. An Iraqi Youth Movement (modelled on Nazi lines) and a local Nazi party were formed. Several newspapers were subsidised so as to render them pro-German in outlook. Special care was taken to influence the Iraqi educational authorities. In 1937, the Iraqi Director General of Education visited Germany, where he was given an official reception. In the following year, an Iraqi delegation attended the Nuremberg Rally. Iraqi students who had reached a certain standard of proficiency in the German language were offered free educational facilities in Germany. German propaganda was even extended to the Iraqi medical profession. In 1937 the Principal of the Royal Hospital and the Dean of the Medical Faculty visited Germany where they were treated to an official welcome. Iraqi doctors who had been trained in Germany were carefully indoctrinated in order to spread Nazi propaganda among medical students. Germany, long before the Second World War, was doing her homework splendidly. She had been stirring up trouble for us for no less than seven years, and with considerable success. They were hoping, planning for and trying to foster a pan-Arab uprising, a holy war against the British which could be turned to their own advantage.

In 1939 when Japan opened a legation in Baghdad, ostensibly to develop trade between Iraq and Japan, it soon became yet another centre of anti-British propaganda. It was all grist to the German mill.

The political events which led finally to the Battle of Habbaniya were, in large part, a direct result of these extensive machinations by the Axis powers, going on *inside* Iraq, although our war with the Axis was well under way. We had imposed severance of diplomatic relations between our ally Iraq and Germany but, amazingly, their activities had not ceased after the outbreak of the war. Admittedly, Dr Grobba became *persona non grata* and had to leave, with his staff; nevertheless, the German propaganda output continued because he had previously and comprehensively transferred the bulk of his organisation into the Italian Legation. Astonishingly, their Legation was not closed, even after Italy declared war upon us. The Germans maintained diplomatic relations with them and for eighteen months after the declaration of war between our two countries the Italians were still working with the Germans directly from Baghdad. They therefore were admirably placed and suited to act as agents and couriers.

All three countries – Germany, Italy and Iraq – were also much aided in their affairs by a notorious and long-standing sworn enemy of Britain, the Grand Mufti of Jerusalem. Immediately after the outbreak of war he, together with a number of Palestinian and Syrian adherents, slipped out of Jerusalem (then within British influence) and arrived in Baghdad where he too found a welcoming haven in the Italian Legation. Thus he was able to direct his vituperative anti-British efforts through the wide-open Italian channels of communication.

Is it to be wondered that our political position deteriorated gravely? The Iraqi Government, supposed to be our ally, was actively plotting against us, in deep cahoots with our enemies – in their country – and still we had taken few, if any, practical precautions. I have tried to discover why the politicians did not find a way of curtailing the treachery of our Iraqi ally, but have failed. I know that the British Ambassador in the lead-up to the troubles was Sir Basil Newton, KCMG. He was replaced on 2 April 1941. He left, with his secretary, saying to those who saw him off that '…although there was some discontent in Baghdad, it was minor and there was nothing to worry about.' This must be described, at the very least, as deeply inaccurate!

He was replaced by Sir Kinahan Cornwallis, KCMG, CB, DSO, a man of great experience with an enviable reputation. He came from a family with many years and members in the Diplomatic Service, had a wartime gallantry award Distinguished Service Order (DSO) – and he was a skilled Arabist. Later, in the Baghdad Embassy, opinions were voiced that the troubles and the battle would never have occurred if Cornwallis had been in place earlier. I was unable to check the validity of that view for it was given to me verbally and I found no papers to support it.

King Ghazi, Britain's friend, was tragically killed in a motor accident in 1939. He was aged twenty-eight. He was succeeded by his infant son, Faisal II, under the regency of his uncle, HRH the Emir Abdullah Illah. The Emir was pro-British, but he was not a strong character. The Nationalist Government was still professing itself pro-British but, with a Regent and a child-King, the reins of power were up for grabs. And the Iraqis were beginning to feel that their military forces, British trained and used to good effect against the tribesmen, were strong and efficient – should they ever be needed.

As has already been noted, Iraq was fundamentally a turbulent country and, naturally, very many of its characters followed that same pattern. One of the most spectacular and colourful of those was a man called Raschid Ali – or, to give him his full name, Raschid Ali el Gailani. He acquired considerable experience as a politician and he developed powerful and burning anti-British feelings along the way. His many-faceted career was full of incident. He, indeed, fully merited the adjective 'turbulent' and, as we meet him many times in this story, let us take a much closer look at him right away.

He began his professional life as a lawyer and in 1921 became a Judge in the Iraqi Court of Appeal. In 1925 he was made Minister of the Interior, but resigned after he was elected as President of the Chamber of Deputies – with most of whom he profoundly disagreed as they were pro-British. Moreover that Chamber, fertile source of impassioned speeches and hot air, did not give him enough raw power. In 1927 he went back to being Minister of the Interior. In 1929, still in that post, he founded the Brotherhood Party – in opposition to the Government in which he had recently served. In 1932, he was appointed Chief Chamberlain and Private Secretary to King Faisal, a Royal appointment with almost unlimited influence.

In 1933, when Prime Minister Naji Shawkat resigned, Raschid Ali stepped smartly into his shoes and took over himself as Prime Minister. This was when he began to co-operate actively with the German Legation in Baghdad, who were only too happy to foster, at the highest ministerial levels, anti-British and pro-German feelings among the Iraqi population. Raschid Ali's prime contact at that period, of course, was *Doktor* Grobba.

That time, he lasted as Prime Minister for only seven months before he found cause to resign yet again. A short period of political limbo followed till 1935, when he reappeared acting both as Minister of the Interior and Minister of Justice. However, when the 1936 military *coup d'état* produced a Nationalist Government pledged to work with the British, it was more than he could stomach and, with Naji Shawkat the former Premier, he skipped off to Syria.

He tried to come back in 1938, but was promptly arrested and deported. However, when Nuri Pasha became Prime Minister once more in 1939, the deportation order was cancelled. Back he came as Head of the Royal Household and, when Nuri Pasha resigned in March, he accepted the Premiership at the request of the Regent, Emir Abdullah Illah. This must have been a matter of expediency because they hated each other's guts.

As mentioned earlier, when we declared war in 1939, the German Legation in Baghdad was closed and Grobba left but this did not stop Raschid Ali adding steadily to his own strength and continuing firmly to develop close relations with our enemies. Through the Italian Legation he worked just as assiduously with the Germans. During the ensuing months his pro-Axis sympathies became steadily and plainly more marked.

By the end of 1940, the internal political situation had become so completely chaotic that yet again Raschid Ali resigned, but only for a few weeks. He did not, however, sit back calmly, waiting. He began to stir up trouble for us yet more actively. He conspired with four colonels of the army, known as 'The Golden Square'. Aided and abetted by his Axis mentors, and using funds received from them in gold, he fostered anti-British feelings everywhere but particularly among the junior officers of the Iraqi Army. The army, and many people in those towns who were subjected to his propaganda, were dividing their sympathies between Germany and their own country. Britain had come to be considered generally as a viper in the Iraqi bosom. Only the rural population remained apathetic, perhaps awaiting some British counter-measures against the rebel Government.

In January 1941, several of the Government Ministers resigned and Raschid Ali swiftly replaced them with sympathisers to the Axis cause.

At the beginning of March 1941 the Prime Minister, Nuri Pasha, resigned and Raschid Ali accepted the Premiership once more, apparently again at the request of the boy-King's Regent, the Emir. This again was a holding operation, prompted by expediency. There was so little love lost between the two of them that at that very moment, the Regent was scheming and plotting with several pro-British Government officials to have Raschid Ali arrested, and perhaps the Golden Square as well, aiming to cut the ground from beneath his feet.

Matters came to a head in two ways simultaneously. First, at the end of March Raschid Ali was almost ready to snatch total power. Second, on 2 April the Regent finally lost his nerve and (perhaps wisely for his own neck) bolted off to the safety of the American Embassy in Baghdad, dressed as a woman. He begged the Americans to take him to the safety of Habbaniya. As it happened, the new British Ambassador, Sir Kinahan Cornwallis, was expected to arrive there that day on the lake, by flying-boat. The American Ambassador, an old friend, was going to meet him so it became quite simple. Ambassador Knadenshue and his wife drove him the 60 miles across the desert to RAF Habbaniya. The British reception party for Cornwallis was somewhat surprised to see a rug moving on the back floor of the American Ambassadorial car. Out from under it came the Regent, dressed in black pyjamas and with a revolver in his hand. The RAF took charge of him and flew him the 300 miles south-west to Basrah, where he was given sanctuary on HMS *Cockchafer* in the Gulf.

An astonishing story concerns the Regent's charge – the boy-King Faisal II. The Regent, Emir Abdullah, left him behind. He must have had considerable faith in an English Nanny. He had entrusted his Monarch, a lad of almost six years old, to the care of one of those redoubtable and Amazon-like protectors. On the other hand, why not? Presumably the Emir felt that precious few of his countrymen would dare to cross, or even rebuke, a British Nanny of those days. In the event, she and the boy were spirited away up to the north of the country. There they stayed during all the ensuing troubles. We know that there was at least one attempt to kidnap the boy, probably for assassination, but it failed. About two months later they returned, unharmed, to greet the British General who led his troops into Baghdad. The boy was spotlessly turned out in white shirt and shorts, immaculately ironed. What a Nanny! Sadly, (post-Nanny) years later one of Raschid Ali's successors had him and his family murdered in the royal palace.

In 1941 we still appeared to think ingenuously that Iraq remained our ally and that Raschid Ali was fomenting some sort of civilian uprising by an uneducated populace. Therefore the events in Iraq were (and for many years continued to be) referred to by the British as 'Raschid Ali's Rebellion in Iraq'. Matters went far deeper than that. As will be shown, Raschid Ali had good reason to believe he was about to embark upon a war to free the entire Middle East from the British, and was confidently expecting German armed and financial support, together with armed uprisings in Egypt, to help him do so. His behaviour was fully in keeping with that plan. The German archives refer to his campaign as 'The War in Iraq'.

In Egypt, 600 miles west of Iraq, the anti-British feelings were just as strong, though not supported at the highest level. It began to reach boiling point far to the south of Cairo, in Mankabad, on the edge of the Nile. A group of young officers discussed Egypt's future. Selfless patriots, idealists, they discussed the need to 'purify' the country. How to rid Egypt of social injustices, the British occupation, political corruption and many such affronts to their aims. They outbid each other in criticisms until the basic question arose – what could be done about it?

A young, tall, shy man spoke up. He was Gamel Abdel Nasser who became President of his country some ten years later. He said: 'We can fight it, and we must fight it – by force of arms if necessary. The way before us is revolution!' He and two others swore on solemn oath to rid Egypt of injustice and oppression. They decided that their *coup* would be timed to take place when the Iraqi attack on the British was well under way.

Rommel and his *Afrika Korps* had been stopped on the Egyptian frontier but Rommel was expecting reinforcements and already had air superiority. We were making plans for our retreat to Alexandria. Our intelligence sources showed that the Egyptian officers were ready to rise against us, and their revolt appeared even more imminent by Raschid Ali's rising in Iraq. When it was learned on 2 May that Habbaniya was under attack, revolt in Cairo seemed to our intelligence to be inevitable.

All the top brass at GHQ Cairo, including General Wavell, thought that Habbaniya would be lost, and that we should have to accept Raschid Ali's terms. We now know that Churchill refused Wavell's pessimistic pleading for a negotiated political solution and insisted on our putting up a fight.

Churchill proved to be wiser than the experts at GHQ in Cairo, who probably were primarily to blame for Wavell's misjudgement. Far more quickly than GHQ had thought possible, the Iraqi Army was at first contained and then routed. The critical moment passed. The signal for an Egyptian Army rising was never given.

Shortly after the Iraq campaign, Wavell was replaced as Commander in Chief Middle East, and Churchill criticised him for his lack of offensive spirit over the Iraqi attack. He was replaced by General Auchinlek who had taken at least some offensive action in sending troops to Habbaniya from India.

No one in Iraq had ever really welcomed Britain as a protecting power, even if she did manage to maintain some form of peace. The history of our presence in Iraq, as in many other parts of the British Empire, was never much better than the tale of an armed truce.

Five
Air Vice-Marshal Smart

Somewhere far, far above me was my ultimate boss, the AOC, Air Vice-Marshal H.G. Smart, OBE, DFC, AFC. I only saw him three times, and one of those was at a distance in the swimming pool. I never managed to speak to him personally. Any instructions from him were all well filtered before they got down the line to me. I knew him to have been a distinguished pre-war aviator. He had been Commandant of the Central Flying School which set the standards for all other flying schools and trained their instructors. He had been at Martlesham Heath, the Gunnery and Air Weapons establishment.

I have the memory of a small, slim man, darting sharp glances at individuals in his audience. He was always well turned out and dapper, as is often the case with men of short stature. He did not project a strong personality but, if you scanned the left side of his tunic, you could see from the brightly coloured medal ribbons that his past had been varied and commendable. Plenty of colour on your chest was referred to as a good 'fruit salad'. 'Reggie' Smart's fruit salad was good.

A cursory glance showed the ribbons of campaigns in which he had served his country. They bore testimony to his war service 'overseas'. A more discerning look near the top of his several rows (four ribbons permitted in each row) would let you pick out the mauve and white diagonal stripes of the Distinguished Flying Cross (DFC). This award is solely for gallantry and bravery when flying in the face of the enemy. Next to it were the carmine and white stripes of an Air Force Cross (AFC). The Air Force Cross is given for commendable and valuable flying in peacetime. So he was a sound and able pilot, as well as a brave one. The first ribbon of all was an OBE, an Officer of the Order of the British Empire, and we servicemen believe that the military Orders of the British Empire are considerably tougher to earn than their civilian equivalents. Reggie had therefore shown he was courageous and competent, in the air and on the ground, in war and in peacetime. All in all, his past service had been good, and merited a record of which he and his family were doubtless justifiably proud.

Smart had begun his career as a regular officer in the Army and, when the RAF came into existence in 1918, he transferred across. He had a neat and tidy mind, and he lived a very full social life. In spite of the RAF Blue or RAF Khaki drill uniform, he remained very much a dyed-in-the-wool type of First World War Army officer by traits and upbringing. He relied heavily on his past Army training – plus what higher authority and the Service books told him to do. He insisted his sections and departments kept up with the jobs defined for them; his organisation, after all, clearly existed to maintain the School's planned output of trained aircrew for the war elsewhere. Diversions were to be avoided for they might have to be paid for in terms of reduced numbers of aircrew coming out of his training-pipeline. Even old and sometimes out-of-date 'orders', 'books', 'laid-down procedures' and 'regulations' – known collectively in the more modern RAF as 'Bull' or 'Bullshit' – were like holy writ to him. He knew they must have been written in the past for some good reason, and they were there to be followed, any apparently necessary divergence from them must of course be cleared in advance by some higher authority. This would have been all very well in peacetime. For a younger generation who were boiling to fight to win against a real enemy, it was anathema.

Behind him was the peculiar ambience of Habbaniya itself. Most of the older officers sent there to run the place in 1941 had been selected because of their character-suitability for a routine task. They liked to produce an effective, efficient and regular output. And were proud to do so. They liked to have precise rules and regulations to be followed, targets to meet, known and understood patterns of work. And, above all, timetables which set out times for work, and times to stop. It left free time to go swimming, sailing, playing tennis or whatever. There was an atmosphere throughout of 'diversions are to be avoided, for they cause hiccups in our programme'. And, of course, diversions also cut into free time.

If the truth be admitted, Habbaniya was much too comfortable and placid for its own good as a wartime base. It engendered a spiritless attitude of 'We have nothing much to get steamed up about; our task – for it is clearly laid down – is to feed a war, which is the direct business of someone else, a thousand miles away.' Many of those older men who should have been in the lead, to use an ancient wartime phrase, 'lacked fire in their bellies.'
This lack of urgency, even in 1941, was mirrored by the Middle East operational centre itself, in Cairo. As far as they were concerned, Iraq was placid; the Mediterranean was dynamite and the Japanese dragon had not yet reared its ugly head. There should be few problems that Iraq Command (by itself or with some help from India) could not handle. Maybe some of the indigenous populace might be disposed to riot, or to stage some form of rebellion, but there were plenty of aircraft able to make a show of force, even if some could only make a noise. Iraq, therefore, had to take a back seat.

In retrospect, Whitehall had been given plenty of intelligence warnings of Raschid Ali's anti-British intrigues, and his requests for direct help from the Axis powers since September 1940 – mainly through decrypts of the Italian diplomatic traffic to Teheran and Baghdad. It was also well known that in Iraq the Italians, the Japanese, the Grand Mufti of Jerusalem and the Germans were *all* involved in anti-British scheming. On the other hand, there were comparatively few reports to really shock them, such as whether or how seriously Germany was responding to Raschid Ali's pleas. So, as our resources in the Middle East were desperately stretched, neither then nor later did Whitehall discuss what detailed steps to take in the event of a severe internal crisis in Iraq. One is forced to conclude that they continued to think any problem there could be treated as 'a local civilian uprising'.

Hence, in early 1941, Whitehall made what appears now to be an amazingly inept decision. Less than one month before the political and operational situation in Iraq began to explode, they switched responsibility for Iraq from Middle East to India. They gave four main lines of (with hindsight) specious reasoning to justify this change.

First, they judged that Germany was *incapable* of mounting in the near future an airborne and serious threat in Iraq, because of her other commitments. (Unlikely perhaps, but by no means incapable).

Second, Middle East Headquarters had two other main campaigns to cope with, in Greece and in the Western Desert, with another apparently certain in Crete. (Likely, yes, but doubtful that they could ever have been stopped if they had gone for Iraq through friendly Syria instead of to Crete. Iraq with all our oil was by far the greater danger).

Third, a belief that any operation in Iraq would be of minor importance. (Frankly, not so. The campaign proved to be critical).

Fourth, in the event of assistance being needed, Iraq was not much further from India than it was from Egypt. (Factually incorrect. India was more than twice as far away, and approachable only by air or sea).

Whitehall took those four parlous elements together as sufficient to justify the transfer of Iraq Command out of the Middle East, and India Command was given that baby to hold on 8 March 1941.

To be fair, it must not be supposed that the British Intelligence services knew it all in detail, and that the Chiefs of Staff ignored the advice. Warnings indeed there were but they did not indicate that a truly critical situation might soon be upon them. Intelligence generalised matters in the sense that they advised all was not well. Nevertheless the decision to switch Iraq to the India Command was most surprising. As early as January 1941 the Foreign Office had warned the Chiefs of Staff that the position of the Regent was deteriorating, because of Raschid Ali's continued connivance with rebellious Iraqi Army colleagues after his Government had resigned.

In the ensuing two months, both before and after the transfer to India, there was a stream of warnings that all was not well in Iraq. The last was as late as 27 March, just as the pro-British Iraqi authorities were preparing to arrest Raschid Ali's army supporters. In hindsight it seems hardly credible that, although the Regent had fled to the British in Habbaniya on the 31 March, the *coup* by Raschid Ali three days later and his declaration of supreme power as 'Chief of the National Defence Government' caught Whitehall unprepared. Moreover, few (if any) of those intelligence warnings seem to have landed on the desk of the Air Officer Commanding RAF Iraq, Air Vice-Marshal Smart.

The General Officer, Commander-in-Chief in Cairo was General Wavell and the Air Officer, Commander-in-Chief in Cairo was Air Marshal Longmore. They, doubtless were looking over their shoulders towards the Western Desert, Greece and the threat of Crete. They knew that Iraq had been dickering with the Germans since 1933 so, what was new? Their policy for the Iraq Command all the way through, transmitted to Smart, was to negotiate, negotiate, negotiate – and don't cause waves.

So, the story that follows, as from the date 2 April 1941, must be seen in the light of a British strategy based on a belief that Iraq would have no serious problems – and, anyway, it was India's baby. Whatever difficulties there might be would assuredly be less grave than the Mediterranean situation. Negotiation was the order of the day.

As Chief of the National Defence Government, Raschid Ali redoubled his machinations with the Germans, through the Italian Legation. The field for him was a fruitful one because Herr von Ribbentrop, Minister for Foreign Affairs in Germany and doubtless briefed by the wily Dr Grobba, had noted Raschid Ali's seizure of power in Iraq. He was at that very moment expressing his firm views in Berlin that a strong force should be sent. They should help the Iraqi Nationalist forces to oust Britain, as soon as it was possible to do so.

We now know that Smart had had for a number of years an RAF intelligence staff, in his Headquarters at Habbaniya, dealing largely with political matters. It is recorded that they gave him no indication whatsoever that Raschid Ali's intentions were deadly serious. Starved of political forecasting due to their gross inadequacy, Smart was in no position to thump the table hard enough to get suitable action. But now, we can see that somebody should have done so.

After Raschid Ali's *coup*, and even though India was his superior Command, Smart begged the Commander-in-Chief, Middle East, on 6 April to give immediate consideration to the matter of sending reinforcements, both air and ground, to Iraq. However, due to the situation in Libya, the German attacks in Yugoslavia, Greece, and the likelihood of a campaign in Crete, the considered view of General Wavell and Air Marshal Longmore was that Iraq's priority was too low, and that nothing would be spared. Smart's hopes were dashed.

The unfortunate Smart, in virtual ignorance of the situation's gravity and having been refused any RAF aid, felt that he nevertheless should do something practical, in case there was trouble. But what should that action be? His main weakness was that, securely tucked away in his sheltered and comfortable training domain, he had never truly come around to the rough and tumble of conflicts in this modern war. His Army background had trained him to accept decisions as handed down to him. He was distanced from the ugly but necessary determination to catch-as-catch-can – and the devil take the hindmost. He was not supported by the tough sentiment of 'All is fair in Love and War'. Either from nervousness of political repercussions and causing waves, or from misjudgement, the several directives he issued to the Flying Training School were very limited in their scope; the only preparations he would accept were such as would not have much effect on the FTS's planned training programme. He was a very proper gentleman.

Wing Commander Paul Holder, whom we met in an earlier chapter, was his Senior Administrative Officer and he had no such scruples. He dreamed up what he believed to be a splendid idea for putting pressure on Raschid Ali and his henchmen. It sprang from the fact that it was well known in the higher levels of our command that all the upper-echelon Iraqis were busily salting away large sums of money, filched from public funds and diverted into personal accounts. Paul trotted in next door to see the great man.

'Sir,' said Paul politely, 'I have thought up a simple scheme by which we can require the rebel Raschid Ali to do anything we want, with no air-operations, nor any loss of life.' Smart raised his eyebrows, and smiled inquiringly. 'I have found that all Iraqi bank-notes are printed by Messrs Waterlow, in Britain, the famous printers of currency for many, many countries. With some co-operation from Whitehall we could tell Raschid Ali that if he does not stop intriguing and behaving contrarily to what we wish from him, we would fly over Baghdad and all the major cities in Iraq, dropping unlimited quantities of banknotes. Specially printed for us by Waterlow's. Real bank-notes, not forgeries. On the proper paper. Of every denomination there is.' Smart frowned. Paul went on, 'Then, as he will readily recognise, almost overnight the Iraqi currency will become valueless. He is no fool, and he will instantly see that all the vast personal fortune that he has amassed would have evaporated. And so also those of his confederates, who would then be ready to do him a severe injury. We would be in complete control.'

Paul sat back and waited for the applause. Smart leaned forward, shock and surprise shining from his face. 'Holder,' he said in tones of utter disapproval, 'we couldn't possibly do such an unacceptable thing. It wouldn't be cricket!' As Paul commented to me later, 'What a frame of mind with which to try and run a war!'

Smart's first requirement was to mount a 'Demonstration Flight'. He must have been guided by thoughts that he was dealing with uneducated tribesmen – potential rioters and local civilians shouting slogans – who would be awed by his 'iron birds' thundering through the sky. 'Quantity' was his byword.

On 6 April his orders went out. On 7 April the camp became like an ant's nest. It certainly made a change from routine instructing, and the formation flying was going to be fun. Everything that we could fly was to be in the air next morning, under the training heading of 'practice flying.'

Pilots were the limiting factor. The final collection was as motley a crowd as the aircraft they flew. All instructors took part, of course. Plus a few of the more advanced pupils. And a couple of Greek pilots who were there to oversee some Greek students. And some more bodies came out of Headquarters. Forty-eight pilots we managed to find, and so forty-eight aircraft flew. Several different types were chosen – thirty-two Harts and Audaxes, thirteen twin-engined Oxfords and the three Gladiator biplane-fighters. Those out-of-date fighters, of course, were not flown by fighter-pilots. They were only there because they had been superannuated from the Western Desert theatre as being beyond practical use in a fighting role. They were kept as a sort of flying sports-car for Headquarters officers to use for any local travelling – and also it gave them some entertaining flying practice to keep their hands in.

This great gaggle – it deserved no better description – took the air on the 8 April. As may be imagined from the comparatively unpractised rag, tag and bobtail in the pilots' seats, the quality of the formation itself was terrible. There were five flights in all. One each of Oxfords and Harts, and two of Audaxes, all cruising at the same speed and, God willing, in the same direction. The three fighters, flying faster, had a roving commission and swooped around, above and below the main formation. Fortunately, none came into collision. The whole of this lot traipsed back and forth near two local villages called Ramadi and Fallujah. 'Near' is the accurate word. Smart was taking great care not to have us fly over the townlets themselves, in case it might be considered a warlike act and our allies, the Iraqis, might be affronted. It could therefore be politically undesirable. The mere sight of the machines, he must have assumed, would demonstrate British air might and impress the populace sufficiently to cause them to abandon all ideas of rioting, or being another kind of nuisance.

The demonstration flight had another consequence – for the School. It had cost us more than a day's training flying. We were immediately ordered to re-double our efforts so as to make up the loss of training hours.

We know now that Hitler had long been hoping for and trying to trigger an uprising against the British throughout the Middle East; a spreading war so that they might join in at minimal cost, ostensibly as the saviours of Islam. Raschid Ali's ambitions, therefore, marched perfectly in step with those of the Axis. On 8 April Ribbentrop's German Foreign-Affairs department gave the Nationalists in Baghdad a long-hoped-for letter, *guaranteeing* German military and financial support 'as far as possible in case of any war undertaken by the Arabs against the British for their freedom.' Raschid Ali believed this letter from the Germans was their solemn promise.

The existence of that letter seems to have been a well-kept secret for it does not appear in British records and, judging from later actions and inaction's on our part, it cannot be credible that it was known to Smart, to the British commanders, or to the Foreign Office. In fact, General Wavell, Army Commander-in-Chief Middle East, told Whitehall the very next day, 9 April, that he could not spare any troops for Iraq, and Whitehall did not demur or make comment.

So, Smart had no idea that his demonstration had taken place the day before that letter arrived and, accordingly, our perambulating training aircraft did not cause a moments hesitation to any Iraqi and it had been entirely valueless. Poor Smart. He had taken such care over our 'maximum effort.'

After Middle East had refused his request for military support, Smart turned to India and that Command reacted positively. Some 400 infantrymen of the 1st Battalion of the Kings Own Royal Regiment had already sailed for Singapore. They were turned round, to head the other way. They were due to land at Basrah, on or shortly after 14 April. In retrospect, perhaps they were lucky men, not to have found themselves in Singapore, to be killed by the Japanese or incarcerated in their prisoner-of-war camps a few months later.

400 soldiers of the KORR was hardly a significant force, so Smart again sought Middle East's help. He asked for one modern bomber squadron and a modern fighter flight to be based at Basrah – in case Raschid Ali decided to cut up rough and oppose the troops' disembarkation. By this time, Air Marshal Tedder had taken over from Air Marshal Longmore. He was a much more positive individual and his reactions reflected it. He thought that the prospect of Raschid Ali resorting to active opposition to the landings was virtually negligible but, nonetheless, he felt that Smart's request was reasonable. He agreed to send a reinforcement of nine Wellington bombers and six fighters. 'Modern' fighters, however, could not be spared and were not to be forthcoming; the six more fighters to be sent would be time-expired Gladiator biplanes from the Western Desert. This would bring Smart's force of fighters up to nine and provide him with a proper threat to quell potential Iraqi dissidents.

Before these machines left, however, Air Ministry in London perked up and decided to put in their two cents worth – in a *negative* direction. They disallowed Tedder's proposals. They could not understand, they said, how he could spare them from the battles in Greece – particularly as he was not expecting any opposition from Raschid Ali.

Moreover, they added, Smart had eighty-four machines which he could use if necessary.

More cock-ups. Eighty-four machines? Whatever might or might not then have been the overall background to the Iraq situation as seen in London, the planners and decision-makers in the Air Ministry were getting their sums and judgements monumentally wrong. Firstly and factually, by counting numbers in paper records, Smart might have been shown to have eighty-four airframes with engines on his books. But, a high proportion of those were trainers, unarmed and unable to carry any weapons at all. Secondly, he had nothing like enough pilots to fly them all. Thirdly, there were intelligence reports available within Air Ministry (though they were not divulged to Smart) indicating that some form of warlike reaction from Raschid Ali was becoming daily more likely. Fourthly (and judgementally) their statement leaves one with the stunning, though logical, deduction that the authors were assuming any potential enemy opposition would not be much above the level of peasant-farmers, armed with muskets and spears – upon whom an unarmed aircraft might have had some effect. It ought to have been plain to the meanest intelligence that this would easily be very, very far from the truth. This was highlighted by the fact, to take one example only, that we ourselves had attached several British officers to the well-equipped and modernised Iraqi Army and to their Air Force, as instructors and advisers to train them in today's warfare.

On the other hand, in spite of those danger-flags, Habbaniya's situation seemed, to our wishful-thinking planners, to be less serious than it really was. Post-war British Intelligence records in London show that they were compounding their errors. They said that Raschid Ali was known to be in collusion with the Axis, yet calmly added (wrongly) that there was 'no firm evidence of a military understanding between him and the Axis powers'. This totally erroneous British intelligence assessment had been deduced from the decrypt of a diplomatic telegram from the Italian Minister in Teheran; it said there was no assurance that Raschid Ali's '*coup d'état* had any anti-British character'. That evidence being so ludicrously misread leads to only one logical supposition, now; that is, that our high-priced-helps really believed that reaction by Raschid Ali and the Iraqis would take the form of a low-risk revolt or rebellion.

How wrong they were! That Italian telegram was so far from fact that it even makes one wonder if it was a deliberate red herring lodged upon us by the enemy. All in all, Iraq stayed well down on the priority totem pole. Then, and for the next twenty years in all official British records, the action of 1941 was played down as a 'rebellion' – which by definition is a civilian uprising. The Germans, on the other hand, bluntly call it a 'war', which is a military conflict.

On top of all that, presumably we failed to appreciate that Raschid Ali was under considerable pressure from his own pro-Axis senior army officers, who were becoming very restive. They wanted, and the sooner the better, to throw the British out – lock, stock and barrel. We know that the majority of Arabs in all countries were convinced that Britain was finished and that Germany would be victorious eventually. We also know, from later intelligence reports that they had told Raschid Ali quite clearly that if he did not move against the British in the very near future, they would get rid of him. He assuredly would have presumed assassination to be selected as the most effective – and permanent – method of ensuring his departure from the political scene.

On 16 April, the British Ambassador Sir Kinahan told Raschid Ali that we, availing ourselves of the provisions of the Treaty, would be disembarking troops at Basrah in the immediate future. As Raschid Ali had accepted the obligations of the Treaty when he assumed office, he could only agree – unless he was prepared to offer armed resistance which, without Axis support actually in the country, was too drastic a step. He did not miss the opportunity, however, to remind Sir Kinahan firmly that the terms of the Treaty were for passage of troops through, and not to have them stay in the country. The Ambassador, of course, was ignorant of Raschid Ali's belief in his position of considerable strength; he had, in his pocket as he spoke, the written guarantee from the Germans to provide financial and military help in an armed conflict.

The Iraqi Cabinet and Defence Council debated the matter the next day at a joint meeting. It was decided that permission should be given for the disembarkation, but that no further troops should be permitted to land until after the first lot had gone.

On 17 April a small advance party from the 400 KORR was flown into Basrah from India by Douglas DC2 and Valentia aircraft of No. 31 (India) Squadron. These were then promptly flown on to Habbaniya. The seaborne convoy duly arrived the next day, 18 April, and the disembarkation of the main party took place without incident, under cover of some of our aircraft. They were flown into Habbaniya a day or two later.

Although Raschid Ali had given formal permission for the soldiers to arrive, he was far from content. More, he became downright enraged when it was apparent that the air-transported advance party was staying in the country, and not passing through as set out in the Treaty's terms.

That same day he told the Axis, through the Italian Legation, that he considered it an Act of War by the British against Iraq and therefore he asked the Germans for the monetary aid and military force which their Foreign-Affairs department had promised only ten days earlier. As a *quid pro quo* he promised in return to make available *all* the airfields in Iraq, for unrestricted use by any German and Italian forces which might come to his aid. The use of 'all' is particularly important, for it would include Britain's main base, Habbaniya. This would undoubtedly have caused a vertical breeze-up in many Allied Embassies and Headquarters, had it been known.

On 21 April, the Iraqi Ministry of Foreign Affairs sent a note to our Embassy. It stated that in line with the decision of the Iraqi Cabinet and Defence Council, no further British troops were to be landed at Basrah until the force which had arrived on the 18th had passed the frontier on its way out of the country, in accordance with the Treaty.

By this time, things were obviously hotting up in Baghdad. Their radio broadcasts and rebel propaganda were becoming increasingly anti-British and indicated that some form of attack on Habbaniya might be in the offing. The School started daily reconnaissance of the roads to the east and west of the camp. We had no inkling as to what form attack – if any – might take.

I, flying an Oxford, was sent to use my earlier photographic-survey experience in India, taking pictures of Raschid airfield in Baghdad to make a modern photo-mosaic map as a precaution. It was unnerving, to say the least, sitting in a lightly built wooden aeroplane, making a series of straight runs, backwards and forwards, forwards and backwards, over the city. It felt like walking down Piccadilly with no trousers on. However, although the Iraqi Air Force must have watched me, very closely, they did not attack or try to stop me, as had been half expected back at Habbaniya.

There were some more troops already on their way by sea from India. This was a small number of ancillaries to the first convoy. In spite of the Iraqi note of 21 April refusing permission for any more troops to be landed, Army Headquarters wished to go ahead and disembark them. On the 23rd, Sir Kinahan formally notified Raschid Ali of this intention. Raschid Ali, still believing of course that he was speaking from a position of strength, bluntly told the Ambassador that any such disembarkation would be taken as an Act of War by the British against his country.

He went further. Bearing in mind that he had promised Germany to free all airfields for Axis use, and having had as yet no positive reaction to his plea of 18 April for Axis help, he repeated on the 26th his request for German forces. He added that he expected his first *military* contact with British forces would come in three or four days – which, in fact, was precisely what occurred. However, there was still no positive German reaction to the impassioned Iraqi entreaties.

On 28/29 April, the second convoy with British troops arrived at the head of the Persian Gulf under air protection from our elderly machines and from HMS ships *Yarra*, *Cockchafer* and *Falmouth*. The Foreign Office in London had authorised the use of force to protect them if necessary, but none was required. The convoy proceeded up the Shatt-el-Arab river to Basrah and the contingent of troops disembarked without incident.

Raschid Ali in Baghdad acted promptly in response to this flagrant disregard of the note from his Ministry of Defence, and his warning to Sir Kinahan himself. First, he asked the Germans, on that day, for 3million Iraqi Dinars and told them that he was about to move. Second, on the 29th, he told the British Ambassador that he would not tolerate this arrival of further British troops.

To our greatest good fortune, the Germans at this point in time had no direct means of influencing Iraqi activities or policies, and the Iraqi approach was unwelcome. In addition, they were acutely embarrassed by Raschid Ali's requests. Their Russian campaign – code-named *Barbarossa* – loomed over their war-horizon and they did not want any involvement in Iraq, yet. They reckoned that contact should be renewed later. So they took no action – which, in the end, gave us breathing space and saved our bacon. Another strategic cock-up, by the enemy this time.

Our Ambassador, because of the increasing tension, thought it prudent to seek Raschid Ali's permission to evacuate women and children from Baghdad to Habbaniya. Raschid Ali gave his permission, without adding that he would start sending out from Baghdad, that same night, an overwhelming force to surround our base. So, for the women and children, it might well have been 'out of the frying pan into the fire.'

It was quickly discovered that there were far too many British wives and children to be evacuated from Baghdad with a mere snap of the fingers, as it were. A substantial number would have to remain in the Baghdad frying pan. Arrangements could be made for the wives of the British Embassy personnel, but there were many more whose husbands worked for firms, contractors and organisations in the city and its environs.

Ambassador Knadenshue came to the rescue. Although the United States was still neutral, and our fracas with Germany and Iraq was no concern of his, he flung open his Embassy gates and welcomed in the Brits – over 150 of them. It must have placed a substantial load on the American Embassy staff and facilities, having that number to accommodate, protect and feed – and it would turn out to last for a whole month!

It is astonishing to learn, now, that at the point when we inside Habbaniya could actually see a well equipped armoured force of the regular Iraq Army – as opposed to local rioters brandishing staves and muskets – it was also the unlucky Reggie Smart's *first* knowledge of Raschid Ali's true intentions. So much for the political intelligence section in his own headquarters!

Back in Egypt and London, it was only after a strong force of the Iraqi Army had actually laid siege to Habbaniya that Whitehall accepted that responsibility for Iraq Command had better revert from India to Headquarters Middle East. And only then – during the first week of May – did they give effect to that decision. Additionally General Wavell was firmly required by Churchill to find and prepare an army column to go and rescue Habbaniya. It was just about Wavell's birthday and he indicated it was a lousy birthday present, considering all the other campaigns he had to handle as well.

If the Germans had profited from the chances handed to them by Raschid Ali and our own numerous and monumental strategic cock-ups, Habbaniya would have been in German hands long before the relieving column from the Middle East could have reached it.

Smart was very unlucky in having to undergo such a harrowing experience, at Habbaniya, and particularly towards the end of his valuable Air Force service.

Six
Preparations

My background had been an incredibly lucky one. Mad about flying (always have been) I had broken upon my first surprised squadron at the age of nineteen. Almost at once I was sent to India to undertake many tasks and, best of all, several of them took me away, to work on my own, at some outpost landing-ground with one mechanic who was also my crewman – me, my aeroplane, my colleague, a supply of fuel and oil in cans, and a box of tools. On my own for perhaps a week or two, except for a daily visit by another aircraft bringing the food and supplies we had asked for the previous day. With luck, there was not even a telephone to cause us trouble. It was fun. I was given masses of responsibility for my age, and I loved it. I must admit to becoming a somewhat independent cuss, and rather big headed. I collected a couple of 'campaign medals' for the tribal peace-keeping operations that came my way, also a stunning collection of photographs from flying among Himalayan mountains stretching up far beyond the eternal snows and far higher than I could reach, having no extra oxygen supply. I got on pretty well with most people, but was not always popular with my superiors when I insisted on going my own way.

That went on until Hitler's war broke out, and I was sent to Singapore, to defend that island against any Far Eastern enemy. Luck again. I came out and went to Egypt shortly before the Japanese came in to kill me quick, or take me prisoner and work me to death. The rapid growth of the RAF, in order to try and beat Germany, caught me right behind the shoulder-blades and propelled me into commanding No. 55 Bomber Squadron at the giddy age of twenty-four.

My squadron was all on its own, under canvas, at a landing ground called Fuka, a couple of hundred miles from Cairo. I was Station Commander, Squadron Commander, father-confessor, judge and jury, briefing-officer, formation-leader – and de-briefing officer. My boss, a First World War Canadian ace, lived under canvas about twenty miles up the road. He called in on the telephone for our results each evening and gave me my bombing details for the next day. Being twenty miles away, he pretty well left me on my own, most of the time. It was, above all, fun – if that is a good word for a deeply satisfying occupation which was progressing well. Within our limits, we felt we were truly helping our country in the war. Having a dozen bombers and 350 men as my sole responsibility was terrific. We got a hell of a lot of raids done, and we lost very few crews. I became even more big headed.

I was given a medal, the Distinguished Flying Cross; I was pleased but not especially excited. I felt that I had just been doing the job, for King and Country, for which I had been paid and trained over many years. I was in effect part of an insurance policy, and my country was justifiably cashing in on the premiums paid. A dangerous job, admittedly, but more or less routine and not meriting the tag of being 'special' or 'distinguished' so far as I was concerned. It was the same for nearly all of my friends and associates. If you were lucky, you lived. I felt slightly hypocritical at wearing the medal-ribbon. You may agree with those sentiments or not, as you please – it's how one felt at the time.

There was one aspect, however, to which I will admit now, but would never have done so then. The 'mental stress' of doing my utmost to keep my crews alive, when many highly trained enemy pilots and gunners were trying their hardest to kill them, began to take its toll. When I failed, and lost someone, the result for me was agonising. Writing letters of condolence to their nearest and dearest, then I would be gripped by nightmares or insomnia. Waking up in cold sweats. Worst of all, a growing and gnawing fear of people thinking me scared, frightened – which, in my heart, I was. I drove myself to continue. No friend or acquaintance could be permitted to think I was lacking guts, or not up to the job.

At last the docs said: 'Out! For a rest. Go!' I protested vehemently that I was still plenty fit enough to lead many more daylight-bombing-raids than the roughly fifty 'ops' that I had so far notched up. But I was sent packing – to Habbaniya.

I flew myself in to Habbaniya on 3 April – the very day that Raschid Ali's *coup* should have caused a great commotion amongst our high-ups. I came for an enforced rest from operational flying – to fly quietly for a while, without the stresses of danger. I brought my dog with me. He was a dachshund, known generally at the time (from their long bodies) as a 'German-sausage dog'. With typical simplistic RAF humour he had acquired the name of Frankie – derived from frankfurter. He was a present from a girlfriend in Cairo and came everywhere with me. Pets were not supposed to fly in RAF aircraft – but there was a war on, and no one on the operational side paid much attention to such lesser rules.

My job: To chauffeur pupils round the desert on navigation exercises, to run a flight of twenty-seven wooden machines, unarmed except for a rear-machine-gun in a perspex dome, for training. They could also carry a camera, looking downwards to plot the fall of practice-bombs. Big deal! Not exactly an inspiring job, after commanding my squadron.

My life was now cocooned from all semblance of hostilities. Everything was calm. I was fed up and felt I was not earning my keep. There were some rumours of a potential rebellion sixty miles away in Baghdad, but it was apparently not serious, just a local uprising. No one paid much attention. Everybody from the Air Vice-Marshal downwards carried out their normal duties, blissfully careless of any dangerous situation in brew. A chap called Raschid Ali was mentioned – a rabble-rouser or something. I had heard it all before, in India. Nothing ever happened unless the politicians got steamed up.

I found I had two direct bosses. The senior one, and definitely a bit distant from me as a mere Squadron Leader, was the CO of the School. He was John Savile, a Group Captain, nicknamed 'Butcher' for his fierceness at insisting on that petty discipline known everywhere as Bull, and for mercilessly failing pupils-in-training for the slightest misdemeanour. He had been an Army officer, a Gunner, before he transferred to the Royal Flying Corps in the First World War, and therefore was probably in his early forties. Perhaps seared by his experiences, he had grown old before his time. As was common with First World War veterans in those days, he never flew. In accord with the tightest early military discipline he followed rules and regulations slavishly. In this respect he marched excellently with his boss, AVM Smart. He passed all orders and instructions, both Smart's and his own, usually in writing, to me through *my* immediate boss.

My immediate senior was the Chief Flying Instructor. The CFI was a much younger, livelier and more understanding individual, Wing Commander C.W.M. Ling. He was known, to one and all, as 'Larry'. We took to each other quickly because (as far as the Butcher would allow) he was not regulation-bound. He drove himself and his juniors straight towards achieving productive and necessary results. He was disinterested in merely following, for tradition's sake, some path or other which had been specified from above, since time-immemorial, as a suitable and decorous way to proceed. He said directly what he wanted, worked himself and his juniors damned hard, but fairly, got what he asked for and was always ready to listen to ideas. Maybe he was a bit of a reactionary at heart, like me.

In this peaceful backwater of a training unit, I did not expect to be a blue-eyed-boy. Nor was I. For openers, I was not even a qualified flying-instructor. In their eyes, merely a stooge pilot. Furthermore, I compounded my problems by being young, enthusiastic, and somewhat smug after my extensive recent war experience. To the junior pilots the fact that I already had a decoration and two campaign-medals made me an object of envy. To the more senior veterans, I was an upstart. My war-inspired credo 'Results first; rules second' was an unwelcome thorn in the side of the more placid top brass; it made waves. I merited, in their view, being placed under severe restraint – frequently. An opinion which I can now see was largely justified. Luckily for me it did not occur. Perhaps it was because they felt it would have been even more disruptive for them.

The screw was given another twist when, not very long after my arrival, the even tenor of their training world began to be progressively disarranged by that uprising in distant Baghdad. The tensions there became steadily more apparent. They saw potential disturbance to life at Habbaniya. To make it worse, they could see the obvious delight of the younger element – including me – at the possibility of some excitement. The young and junior flying instructors, full of spirit and raring to go, were woefully frustrated at being cooped up, divorced from the war, and they longed for a chance to 'have a go' at the enemy – any enemy. However, down in the hangars we had our strict orders, to keep up with the training programme.

This did not stop me, one of the simpler pilots, so to speak, giving thought to how we might enhance our striking power, should things turn nasty. There was no sense in having aircraft that could not be used to their maximum capacity if needs be. Even the forecast of ignorant peasants in their thousands could be highly dangerous, and the Iraqis were plainly a substantial cut above that. Who knew what might happen? After all, everyone knew the Iraqis, over and above the peasants, had both an army and an air force, largely British-trained – so they should by no means be judged as unintelligent.

I began, with Larry Ling, from the obvious start point that if the camp was besieged by a mob, whether large or small, we should not be able to use the airfield. It did not even have a protecting fence around it. The fence only surrounded the domestic and technical areas. There had to be an aircraft-parking-area, inside the camp, where we could lodge the machines safely. The narrow tree-lined roads didn't have the width to tow or taxi the aircraft along them, so it had to be big enough for us, with care, to fly them in or out as necessary. The solution was simple, even though it caused a certain amount of tooth-sucking among the sporting die-hards. With the accord of our bosses, the cherished polo-pitch and the golf-course were carefully destroyed and bulldozed flat to make our dispersal ground. Every machine which was unable to make a landing on that little 'airfield' had to be locked away, out of sight, overnight, in the hangars. The remainder were then flown across to the polo-pitch each evening – and back again next morning in order to maintain our normal flying – and thereby keep to our bosses sacrosanct training programme.

Next, what about the training machines themselves? The biggest bomb any of them carried weighed only 20lb. More than half couldn't carry any bombs at all. Demonstration fly-arounds were all very well, but suppose the rebels turned up with some of the machine-guns or modern rifles which they were known to possess. Suppose the Iraq Army took a hand in support? Suppose we needed bigger bombs?

On our own and with Larry's support, we first tackled our seven 'Gordons'. Gordons were designed as biplane bombers, made by Messrs Fairey's, shortly after the First World War. It might have been a splendid modern bomber some twenty years earlier, but it had left the front line many years since. It was so far out of date that it had been relegated to the role of target-towing. It droned around the sky at about 80mph, towing a kind of flag or tubular fabric-sleeve a mile or so behind it on a long cable. That mile was to allow the pupils to shoot live-ammunition at it without, God willing, shooting down the towing Gordon as well. After the pupils had exhausted all their ammunition, a propeller was swung out into the slipstream to spin at the end of a strong metal rod and, turning a winch, it wound the target back in again.

As an aircraft for the Second World War, it was far too old and clapped out but, praises be, it had been designed as a bomber and those seven machines were the only bombers, ancient or otherwise, in the whole place. They had the necessary fittings to bolt on what were called 'Universal' racks, which could carry big bombs – twelve times larger, at 250lb. All the necessary, but unused, release gear was there, so any change of role would be simple and could be made quickly. We made a trial-run with each, checking that the elderly bomb-release wires could be pulled to let a bomb drop. Now, all we had to do, if the balloon went up, was to take off the wind-driven winches for the towed-targets – bolt on two bomb-racks, load up a couple of 250lb bombs – and away we could go. So far, so good.

Which aircraft next? The nearest we could get to Second World War machines were the 'Gladiator' biplane fighters. We had three which were kept on the shelf for staff-officers to flip around the country, on staff-visits and such-like. All of them had been superannuated from any war theatre. Of course, as the airborne go-karts of the station, no one had provided belted-ammunition for their four machine-guns, mounted to fire forwards between the propeller-blades. No matter. This was not insuperable. We would make the ammunition-belts by hand.

In the station-armoury was a weird and wonderful device like a crazy mincing-machine worked by winding a big handle. You fed in a cartridge which you had slipped into a black metal clip. Turn the handle, once. With a clattering noise it poked the cartridge just the right distance into the clip and shifted it along one slot. Slip a second cartridge in, with another clip. Turn the handle once more. And again. And again. Soon, coming out of the other side of the device would be a properly adjusted belt of rounds, ready for a machine-gun. Not difficult, and it worked – but a slow business. One needed to be careful not to get fingers in the works while a colleague was turning the handle. They would go in, easily, but finger-ends would be a hindrance to the machine-gun later.

We tasked teams of pupils for the job. It was not skilled labour, and it was boring beyond belief, and we only had one mincing-machine. Poor fellows. I said to the first lot, 'We are really sorry to give you this task. It is only because we simply *must* have the belts. It is a vital job for the operations that may come, and we are relying on you to produce the goods – as I know you will.' That evening, one of them made a point of saying to me: 'Sir, I have calculated the consumption. There are four guns on each Gladiator. Every time the pilot touches the trigger-button, they fire off an hour's work in less than ten seconds. *How* many belts did you say you needed?' I gave him the truthful answer which he didn't want to hear; 'We need as many belts as you can possibly make.' He didn't dare say what he plainly was thinking. Somehow I felt my voice lacked conviction for, as I went out of the door, I heard *sotto voce* comments upon my unwedded parentage and what would occur if they came upon me in a dark alleyway. However, they slaved away in shifts of three, willingly. Their muttered threats of what they hoped to do to me no doubt helped them to let off steam.

How about our other aircraft? This would be the start of many frustrations to be overcome, and some satisfactions. I was painfully aware that we had a motley bunch of aircraft, obsolete or obsolescent, suitable only for training in the pure art of flying – otherwise they would have been scrapped. They were either entirely unarmed, or merely lightly armed. What could we do to improve matters? They were all much slower and less 'operational' than those that the Iraqi Air Force had, if they happened to show up at any time.

There were quite a lot of 'Audaxes' and 'Harts'. What about them? In the late 1920s or early 1930s Messrs Hawkers had designed a single-engined, two-seater biplane – a splendid machine for its time. When new it had cruised at about 150mph and it came to be used in many RAF roles and was called by different names. As a day bomber, it was a Hart. It carried two fairly large 250lb bombs and made an ear-splitting noise for it had no exhaust pipes; this allowed it to extract maximum efficiency from its engine. Harts were so easy to fly they were even used as trainers, fitted with dual controls – and exhaust-pipes so that the pupil could hear better what his mentor was saying – and they had no fittings for any armament at all. When it went to sea in an aircraft carrier it became an Osprey and was duly fitted out for its naval tasks, which included bombing. When its role was for Army co-operation duties it came to be called an Audax. It too had exhaust-pipes so that the pilot might be able to hear the feeble radio of those days. It carried eight small 20lb anti-personnel bombs for harassing soldiers, preferably cavalry because their horses got scared and bolted. After service in the debilitating sandy air of the desert, our engines could only drag them along at the mediocre speed of about 120mph. But, essentially, they were all the same basic aircraft and we had about thirty Audaxes and twenty-five Harts. How could we jack up their potential?

I had flown bomber-Harts during four years in India, operating over the North West Frontier Province, with two large and eight small bombs on board. Our Audaxes, of course, were fitted only for the standard 'Light-Series' bomb-racks, to carry the normal eight small bombs totalling 160lbs. So, I reckoned, why not raise our Audax bombing capacity by bolting on 'Universal' racks like the Gordons, instead of the smaller ones? Adjust the bomb-releases to suit and thus carry three times as much explosive! Dead simple. The basic fittings were already in place. Let's do it. I trotted off and explained my proposal to Larry Ling. Larry was delighted and thought the idea was great. He, in his turn, took the idea to the Group Captain.

The Butcher, old fashioned and true-blue to his finger-tips, took out his official notes with their lists of possible Audax loads. Having thumbed through it, he looked up at Ling and said, gravely, 'No; it's not a standard bomb-load as laid down in the manual. It cannot be done, or they would have said so.' He shut the book, indicating that the interview was over, but Larry stayed put. He pressed the Butcher hard and cited me, pointing out that I had a mass of experience on these Hawker-aircraft, carrying that bomb-load – so why not? Butcher was unimaginative as well as adamant. He insisted that I had *not* flown these aircraft with that load. I had flown *Hart* day-bombers, which were not *Audaxes*. There might be differences in the machines, seen or unseen, or in their performance – which we did not know about. It would be wrong to go outside the rules. Larry fought tenaciously and finally Butcher gave in to the extent that Larry could go and talk it over with the engineer officers in Headquarters. He had passed the buck – one level upwards.

The engineers were even more strait-laced and adamant. If something unforeseen should occur, and I had an accident, the chap who had said 'Have a go!' might be held responsible. No middle-aged engineer was going to stick his neck out *that* far! Larry, finally by sheer persistence, got the buck pushed up yet once more. Up as far as the ultimate bosses – the operational air-staff. They admitted that they could appreciate the advantages in having bigger bombs to use but, as to giving the go-ahead for a trial by me – no. Imagine their fat heads, filled with mental molasses, giving that type of decision for a potential shooting war! But, under Larry's pressure, they did agree that the engineers could send a signal, seeking permission from Air Ministry in Whitehall, London. So the buck was edged upwards again, yet another level higher for this peanut-sized decision.

The engineers' message turned out to be one which to this day sticks in my mind as a classic of wooden-headedness. Even with permission to draft it as they chose, they were not going to risk being held in question, or to ridicule, for proposing something out of the ordinary. They signalled Air Ministry, asking blandly: 'What is the bomb-load of an Audax?'

I have always wondered what on earth its recipient in London thought Habbaniya was playing at? What, in Heaven's name, had moved a bunch of fairly senior officers out there to pose such a wet and fatuous query anyway? Surely, everyone knew the simple and obvious answer was written clearly in the standard Audax manuals? Naturally, the accurate answer came back like a flash: 'The stated bomb-load of an Audax is eight 20lb bombs.' Which of course we all knew already, only too well. The engineers said smugly that authority for our outlandish suggestion had not been given, and they assumed that to be the end of it. Not so; Larry and I were made of sterner stuff.

Larry met me in the Mess and, over first one and then many more noggins in the bar, we held a council of war – in more senses than one – on how to overcome the impasse. We agreed quite quickly that Headquarters, and the Butcher, were being obsessively blinded by bullshit in the face of a political situation which might turn serious. It might not – but who could say? Like Boy Scouts, we should 'Be Prepared'. For my part, the answer was bluntly simple – I knew it would work. Whatever the Butcher might say, I had done over a thousand hours flying on that type of machine, and hundreds of those were for carrying two of the larger bombs *plus* eight of the small ones! I knew full well that as a flying machine it was like an elderly cob from a livery stable. A placid hack, even for the inexperienced, with no vices whatsoever.

To compound our frustration, we knew full-well that Ospreys (also with exhaust-pipes) carried the big bombs for the Royal Navy from those minuscule runways called aircraft-carriers. What a naval pilot could do in an Osprey, *any* old RAF pilot could do in an Audax! With the heavier load than normal, and not forgetting those exhaust-pipes, she might run a few yards further before she could be lifted off the ground, but nothing worse. We could just put on the racks, load the bombs – and give it a whirl.

'Sir,' I said (Larry was a wing commander and I was only a squadron leader, and the niceties had to be preserved) 'do you know that in India we often loaded our Harts with more than double the loads we are now discussing! Of course, as you will realise, we usually concealed those gross overloads from our bosses, mainly because they weren't bombs. We kept quiet in case they forbade it. We lifted the best part of 1,000lb of creature-comforts to our Army colleagues at benighted outposts up in the Himalayas – *and* at high-altitude. Tinned meat, fresh sausages, bananas, oranges, kippers and much more. Even a battery-driven movie projector. And, more often than not, booze. How about gently telling the group captain of those loads, as he is fussing like a wet hen about a mere 500lb?' Larry thought carefully for a bit. I think he disapproved slightly of 'wet hen' being said out loud when speaking of a group captain - *think* insubordinate thoughts about a senior officer, as you wish, but do not *voice* them! Then, grinning, he replied, 'To quote something as contrary to his books as that would truly put a cat amongst the Butcher's pigeons. It would drive him clean up the wall!' And, in sober retrospect, I agreed it would be absolutely true.

It was not after too long or too many beers before we found ourselves in total harmony. I would just load an Audax and go and do it. After the umpteenth noggin we even felt we would be brave enough to approach superiors *afterwards* saying (politely, of course) 'I told you so!'

Nevertheless, although Larry was quite willing, he reckoned that out of courtesy he should tell the Butcher first. Butcher nearly jumped out of his skin. He had had years of conditioning in the old army, required to obey orders without demur, or face a Court Martial – because that was the way it had always been. He foresaw his blameless time as a gunner-officer, then his years in the RFC, and finally in the RAF, all becoming jeopardised by a couple of irresponsible nitwits.

At first it he gave an unequivocal 'No.' Then, as Larry told me later, under more pressure he gave his reluctant agreement, but asked for a written note from Larry, or me, saying that I was making this test flight on my sole responsibility, and in the full knowledge that it was against his wishes and advice. This total clearance of his own yard-arm – at the expense of his juniors – left Larry amazed. Me too, for that matter. Larry flatly refused and it was fortunate that, of the two, the Butcher proved to be the weaker character. Within the hour we had the racks bolted on an Audax, two bombs loaded and, naturally, she lifted off like a sparrow, flew quite happily and landed 'smooth as a baby's bum'. Of course it did; that aircraft of many names had been doing so for years, with or without exhaust-pipes.

Nearly everyone then professed themselves delighted at Larry's 'useful innovation'. We dug out of stores enough Universal racks to create twelve never-before-seen Audax-bombers. With our seven Gordons, this was good news. We now had nineteen bombers at 500lb each. Very satisfying. It was a great pity that it used up our total stock of Universals, so any other Audaxes would have to pig it with the standard load of eight lesser bombs on their normal Light Series bomb-racks.

Now, how about the Hart-trainers? These were fitted with dual-controls in the back seat, used purely for teaching the art of piloting a machine which was a bit heavier than the very light aircraft used by brand-new youngsters from the word 'go'. There were no mountings, cables or levers for any kind of weapons whatsoever, practice or otherwise. The rear-cockpit only had a seat, and controls, for the instructor. We were undaunted. We were sure we could solve the problem somehow.

We were wrong. Although Larry enlisted the imagination and inventiveness of all the instructors, and even the pupils, we only got some of the wildest thoughts and ideas worthy of that most original and famous cartoonist Heath Robinson. We had to admit defeat. There was nothing anybody could dream up that would meet our three criteria – makeable, fittable and flyable. Very irritating; there, lying around, were a couple of dozen aircraft with a useful lifting-capacity, and we could find no way of letting them use it. Their sole job could only be one which entailed swoops and noises.

So we turned to the last remaining type of machine in the School – 'Oxfords', designed in 1934. Those machines were the brainchild of a firm called Airspeed Ltd. In 1933 they built a lightly-constructed single-engined four-seater passenger-monoplane and named it a 'Courier'. It was made largely from wood and plywood. It flew nicely and was a pleasant device from a pilot's point of view. But, it was a commercial flop and the company was strapped for cash. Luckily, they were then taken over by the shipbuilding firm, Swan Hunter – which solved the cash-flow problem. So they grabbed the chance of building a bigger machine, which would have two engines. For economy and speed in production they used as many components from the Courier as possible. So, it too was lightly built of wood and plywood, helped out by a simple metal-skeleton upon which were hung the heavy components, like engines, landing-gear, and so on. Economy went all the way through. The inside fittings were, to say the least, Spartan. Although the selected engines were small and not very powerful, the construction was so light that it could carry no fewer than eight passengers, and a pilot. They called it an 'Envoy'.

When Britain decided to throw everything it had into the pot for defeating Hitler, the Envoy production line was promptly switched to producing a basically similar aircraft for aircrew-training. It was equally light, equally fragile and made of burnable material – plywood – but the war lent urgency, and it wasn't going into battle, so who cared? The crew would be one pilot and one navigator, with three or four pupils in the cabin. A trainee-rear-gunner sat under a sort of Plexiglas conservatory, or cupola, halfway back towards the tail. It also had a Plexiglas nose, through which an embryo bomb-aimer might peer down over his bombsight, releasing practice smoke-bombs with greater or lesser accuracy. The smoke bombs, weighing 9lb each, were carried on normal Light-Series bomb-racks under the belly of the aircraft. All those changes to its shape made it a bit awkward to fly at low speeds. It could be unstable with some very startling and inexplicable twitches at take-off and when nearing touchdown. Sometimes, it was not only the Oxford that twitched.

An Oxford had never for an instant been considered by the RAF as an operational machine – strength and battle-worthiness were of no importance; in its training role it would never, presumably, suffer any in-flight battle-damage. Moreover, when the Air Ministry asked Airspeed for the aircraft to carry eight practice-bombs, that is precisely what they got. A cut-out recess, below the cabin floor, was just big enough for smoke bombs, and nothing else. So, in the Habbaniya Air Headquarters war plans, Oxfords had been written in as being capable only of photography, machine-gunning, and showing-the-flag – which means swooping around to try and look businesslike when you're not. Which, according to their books, was legal and absolutely accurate.

However, there were twenty-seven of them sitting idly by, so what could be done? My practical training at Cranwell before the war led me to spend a lot of time trying to work out how on earth we could fasten, fix, screw, or bolt on two (or better still, four) Universals. Even though we had used up all we had, bespoken for the Gordons and Audaxes, a quick scrounging trip down to Basrah or wherever might produce some more – if I was persuasive enough. The load was not going to be excessive; that much we knew. The basic design was for eight passengers, and they would weigh a little over 1,200lb. Add their luggage on top of that. Four 250lb bombs was much less, even with the racks included. However, even my fitter and rigger had to admit defeat on two counts. First, we couldn't find a practical way to reach strong-points from which we could hang half-a-ton of bombs and racks. Second, even if we solved *that* problem, there was no bomb bay and the aircraft itself was much too low to the ground to get bombs and trolleys underneath for loading

It certainly wouldn't have been difficult to saw away some of that featherweight wooden fuselage, but weakening even further the already lightweight construction might have been too risky, even in a war-situation. My chief technician nearly threw a fit when I put it to him seriously.

So, the best I could do would be to hang eight of the smaller explosive bombs on the Light-Series racks, in place of the smoke-bombs.

Even that was easier said than done. The hole specially made for 9lb smoke bombs, as asked for by Air Ministry, was too small for the explosive ones. With racks in the hole, twenty-pounders wouldn't go on them. Vice-versa; with bombs on the racks, they wouldn't go in the hole. Well, all was not lost; I could see two possible answers. How about sawing some of the plywood away to make the hole bigger, or hang the bomb-racks on to the aircraft differently?

My second idea was the easier to do. Make some short, metal plates a few inches long, with a couple of holes in them, one at each end. Then we could bolt the plates onto the aeroplane, and the bomb-racks on to the plates, that much lower down. So, the explosive bombs on the racks could stick out in the fresh air under the bottom of the fuselage – and why not? This seemed to be the safest, simplest (and quickest) solution. I could even continue top-brass's all-important training programme which they continually demanded of me – using practice-bombs as usual, but on the low-slung racks. Again, why not? Then, if there was a crisis which really came to boiling point, I could switch from training to a war-posture in minutes by merely hanging on eight vicious anti-personnel bangers, instead of the smoke-bombs – on each of my twenty-seven Oxfords.

When I got down to designing the actual fittings, the job turned out to be much easier than I had thought. I found that the noses of the 20lb bombs would go up into the hole quite happily without making any changes to the rack-mountings. It was only the tail-fins that were too long to go right up inside. All we had to do was to lower the back-end of the rack. The bomb's tail-fins would stick out a few inches – and all would be well. And, only two plates needed for each machine, instead of the four I had expected.

I told Larry. He was as tickled as I was with the idea. Dead simple, and quick to make. He went off happily to station workshops, to have them use their cutting and drilling machines to make quickly the hundred plus little metal strips we needed.

Workshops' flung up their hands in horror and acute alarm. They reacted with all the enthusiasm of a young lady finding a snake in her bed. Such a situation was considered neither normal nor welcome. Their total rejection of my plans made matters even more difficult. They flatly declined to make the bits – unless Headquarters first accepted all responsibility for the change of rack-attachment – and change to the aircraft-load as written in the books – and change to its flying-characteristics with these excrescence sticking out – and to waive any responsibility for them, should the bits be used and something untoward occur.

The engineering staff-officers up in Headquarters, when approached, also found a mass of reasons why the idea was a dud. The prime and all-powerful objection raised was that we proposed making an 'unauthorised modification' to the aircraft. What we wanted wasn't allowed for in their books. It was clearly and firmly stated in their Big Black Manuals that such changes could only be agreed by Air Ministry, and *then* only after discussion with the designers and makers of the aircraft! Which was impossible. The

Germans were sitting in France. There was no airmail to England. No way could they get drawings, descriptions and reasons for our suggestion to the Air Ministry in time to be of any good. By the written rules, they were right. A true statement but, considering there could be a shooting war on our doorsteps, an unworthy one.

On top of all that, the technical staff concluded with what they obviously assumed to be the final clincher. We would recollect, which we assuredly did, the fact that an Oxford with the wheels lowered was well known at times to be unpleasantly sensitive at low speeds; these tail-fins projecting – they said – could, perhaps, even throw the machine out of control on take-off or when landing, causing a fatal crash.

My reaction to Larry's account was frustration and pig-headedness. I did not agree with the engineers' fears – provided that the first test-flights were made with great care and delicacy, anticipating possible trouble. I was responsible for all the Oxfords and I saw several points in my favour. An enhanced strike-capacity could be all important for us. Any war is, by definition, a risk-demanding situation anyway. I had just come from a war-theatre where far greater risks were part and parcel of my daily work. So I was in favour of having a go.

'Sir,' I said to Larry, and followed up with my reasons for doing something positive. Larry agreed, and went back to do his best to get some live action. As a result, Headquarters went so far as to send another signal to Air Ministry, describing my idea, and asking them to give permission for it to be used. Air Ministry, however, sent a bland and indecisive reply. This was hardly surprising for London at this time believed that no direct enemy threat involving strike action was expected. Smart had told them he was engaged only in 'prudent local preparations within our normal training programme.' What reason was there for my taking apparently needless risks?

Air Headquarters was firm and unequivocal. Smart echoed the engineers' fears and no one thought that my idea came in any shape, manner or form under the heading of 'prudent'. The answer to Larry was 'No, No, No'. To make doubly sure that no one could be in any doubt this time and that there would be no repetition of the Audax unauthorised flight, they even handed him the decision written down on a piece of paper. Written orders, no less – and he was to arrest me if I disobeyed them.

Larry came back to the hangars frustrated to distraction and we talked. The immediate upshot was that we returned once more to the Mess Bar for another conference. There, we came to a decision worthy of the 'Father of The RAF', Marshal of the Royal Air Force, Lord 'Boom' Trenchard. Many years earlier, that great officer had been pestered by Staff Officers and Politicians to give an immediate answer to some question – which he had declined to give until he was good and ready. The file kept coming back with more and more insistent demands written into it. So he hid it under his office hearth-rug. It was weeks before somebody established that it was missing, and even more weeks before they unearthed it. Finally, Boom came in one morning to find a weeping cleaner who had been arrested (because she hadn't cleaned under the carpet and found it) and scads of RAF Police. They apologised for the intrusion, and assured him that they would punish the miscreant who had put an important and 'Secret' file under his hearthrug. 'Don't bother;' said Boom, 'I hid it there.'

The astounded reaction produced total silence. At last, his voice squeaking with emotion, the senior copper said: '*You* put it there? Sir!?'

'Yes. I was so fed up with being asked fatuous questions, ahead of time, by footling civilian pen-pushers that I made as if I had not heard them. Now, enough time has passed by for me to give them an answer, and I shall do so. Good day, gentlemen.' And, having given the cleaner a comforting pat on her shoulder, he shooed them out.

Larry and I decided that I, like Boom, would be conveniently 'unaware' of the contents of his written orders – which in a way was true for they were still in his pocket. Also, we would maintain through thick and thin that we had never discussed the matter – which was untrue, but who else was to know? Larry would depart hence, with his orders still hidden from me – leaving me in peace to 'suck-it-and-see', on my own.

Knowing that what I was about to do was in direct disobedience of some orders which, according to rumour, Larry might have received – and which I had prudently not asked to see – I took special care not to involve anyone else, particularly the airmen who would cheerfully have helped me. They did not deserve the hammering that would come to them for doing unauthorised work, if I failed in any way.

First, I borrowed tools – drill, bits, punch, hammer, hacksaw, files – and a work-bench. Fortunately, some strip-steel 'fell off the back of a lorry.' Then, drawing on my early Cranwell training in sheet-metal work, I quickly made a prototype set of four fitments. Picture if you will a squadron leader, a pilot, beavering away, cutting metal, drilling and filing at a bench, bolting bomb-racks on to an aircraft and trying out loading them with unfused high-explosive bombs – all by himself with no armourers and mechanics advising or taking part. There was no way that it could be kept secret nor make a pretence that nothing unusual was in the wind. It was fascinating, glancing up from time-to-time at airmen and junior officers keeping a respectful distance. I was reminded irresistibly of those inquisitive and furry little Meerkats of the South African desert which cannot resist popping out of their burrows to sit bolt upright and see what goes on – to disappear again in a trice if ever they become nervous. By the time the job was done, there was quite a sizeable and interested audience of human Meerkats in the background – most of them pretending not to look.

Doing a 'Nelson' and focusing only my sightless eyes on Headquarters' books, rules and procedures, I studied the eight small explosive bombs on the racks, with their tail-fins sticking out. They *looked* all right; they didn't stick out much. So I made ready to fly the beast. If, as I believed, the idea worked, all would be well. If, as the technical chaps feared, the Oxford crashed out of control I wouldn't be around to take the rap anyway.

Inevitably the buzz had spread, like ripples on a pond. And, equally inevitable, the news finally got as far as Headquarters.

I heard later that top-brass became almost apoplectic at this gross breach of Good Order and Air Force Discipline – clear and specific orders, and in writing too, were being flagrantly disobeyed! Luckily, they sent for Larry, and not me. He had a personal and most illuminating interview with the Great Man Himself – Air Vice-Marshal Reggie Smart no less. And the Butcher too had been summoned to be in attendance.

Later, Larry told me that Smart said to him, personally and unequivocally, that by not stopping me at the outset he had conspicuously failed in his duty. If anything happened, such as losing a valuable aeroplane, Larry would be held fully and personally to blame. Now, his clear orders were to find me and stop me in my tracks. Arrest if necessary was mentioned.

Fortunately for us both, all that palaver took some time. While they were fully occupied with themselves, I took off, carefully and without trouble. To my relief the machine flew quite normally, and it landed normally too.

Larry chuckled endlessly as, a good deal later, he filled me in with the whole story. His seniors had been deeply worried at the prospect of losing a valuable Oxford, and having to explain why they had failed to stop it. They appeared quite unconcerned about losing me. I was a bit huffy to learn their sense of priorities, until I saw the funny side. Now, I can accept that they were not wholly unreasonable in the circumstances of that time. It was not the last of the troubles I caused.

When the mushroom cloud of black smoke over Headquarters had settled, and Larry was in good odour again because he had devised such a simple, practical and effective modification, all was forgiven and I was forgotten. Station Workshops were instructed to make another twenty-six sets of four fitments, one set for each of my remaining Oxfords. Considered singly, eight small anti-personnel bombs is not much of a load. Put together, however, it is much better. Remember first that one 20lb bomb carries the same amount of explosive as a 6in shell. And twenty-seven Oxfords could now carry 216 of them, which was about a couple of tons of bombs. Which was much better than none at all. And, with that, an ability to strike twenty-seven extra targets – if the crunch ever really came. It was a pity that Larry's and my most determined efforts could only rustle up a total of ten more machine-guns to spread between the remaining Oxfords.

It seems that there is some truth in the old adage 'God helps them that help themselves.' We had barely finished when Tedder sent us six more most welcome Gladiators from the Middle East. Manna from Heaven! Larry and I pleaded with Headquarters to hang on to their six ferry-pilots too. No matter that they were a motley band of Free-French, Polish, Yugoslav and a couple of Brits. They were warm bodies who could pilot aeroplanes – and we needed pilots desperately. A signal, even, was sent asking permission to do so. Middle East said 'No'. My cries of anguish became louder still, suggesting that we should quite simply hijack them and refuse them a return-flight to Egypt. But, even Larry wouldn't play ball with that hot potato, and Headquarters dutifully sent them away.

This time, our hearts really bled for the poor teams of pupils; that pestiferous mincing-machine was going to become nearly red-hot with work, making ammunition-belts.

Lastly, we added up the aircrews. We had only two bomb-aimers and two rear-gunners, who were on the staff to give general instruction in those skills. So, in case we had somehow to make up complete crews for our aircraft, we began crash-courses in bombing and gunnery for all the pupils. Better an air-gunner or bomb-aimer half-trained than to have a complete ignoramus!

Larry and I took stock. It was highly satisfying. Our fighting force, if needed, was made up of twelve Audaxes and seven Gordons to carry two 250lb bombs each; nine Audaxes and twenty-seven Oxfords to carry eight 20lb bombs each; and, our nine precious Gladiator fighters. But, for Larry and me, our most satisfying feelings came from simple arithmetic. The minor changes we had fought tooth-and-nail to achieve had *doubled* the number of machines which could make an attacking sortie, and *more than doubled* the weight of bombs that they could drop.

Events were to show that our hard-fought struggles to increase the School's strike-capacity succeeded only just in time.

Seven
Coming to the Boil

At 2 a.m. on 30 April 1941, the British Embassy in Baghdad sent a wireless signal to AVM Smart, saying that they had seen and heard large bodies of men, and vehicles, moving out from Raschid Barracks, crossing the bridges and disappearing under cover of darkness in the direction of Habbaniya. Somebody promptly blew the General Alarm, but no one in the rest of the camp knew what it was all about so nothing happened.

Smart's position was horrible. The tale of his problems, doubts, vacillations and indecision as told in the official British record makes fascinating reading. They record his unlucky story quite clearly – if the story of a confused man in a muddled situation merits the description 'clear'.

Up to that moment, all the pressures seemed to have been around Basrah. He had sent Gladiator fighters, Valentia transports and some Audaxes to help and protect the landings of troops there. He, back at Habbaniya, had been pressing on with his normal training tasks, and trying to keep them right up to schedule in spite of everything. On the 29th his orders passed down to us had been to complete a high-pressure day's flying training, to redouble our efforts and try to catch up with time lost. At which we had done our best. The same efforts had been ordered for the morrow, 30th.

On the 30th we all duly reported to the flights as usual, ready to fly our dispersed aircraft back from the polo-pitch and start the training programme set the previous evening. However, unknown to us in the School, the pot had already begun to boil. There, to be seen on the 200ft-high plateau dominating the camp on the far side of the airfield was the Iraqi Army, digging in and with the snouts of their field-guns pointing straight at us. We were somewhat disconcerted, but it came as a far nastier shock to Smart's army-trained system. His Intelligence Office had been so inefficient that they had given him no idea he was to have a military force to contend with, civilian rebels, he was led to believe, were the worst he could expect.

Suddenly and completely unprepared, Smart found himself likely to be facing a maelstrom of ground-based risks within his own back yard – with virtually no ground forces to counter them. Moreover, he was agonisingly aware that he had no clear directives on how to handle such a situation. Indeed, we were all unready to some extent. Down on the camp it rapidly became 'order, counter-order, and disorder.'

Our dawn-reconnaissance Audax landed back and the pilot reported that the plateau was crawling with something over 1,000 troops, with field-guns, howitzers and armoured vehicles. They were in a sort of semi-circle, less than 2,000 yards away, overlooking the camp. And more could be seen arriving on the approach road. We also could see them clearly from the hangars, with or without binoculars. In a sort of alarmed disbelief we wondered 'What in hell do we do now?'

The worst thing, so far as we were concerned, was the pilot's report of enemy field-guns, howitzers and armoured-vehicles up there, for in modern terms we had none. Some of the Iraqi guns were set up to cover the airfield at point-blank range (2,000yds for a field-gun *is* point-blank range!) An Iraqi light anti-aircraft pom-pom gun covered the approaches. Iraqi armoured cars and light tanks were being parked within a few hundred yards of the airfield's edge. Against that lot we only had half-a-dozen RAF armoured-cars which, during the First World War, had been created from civilian Rolls-Royce chassis with some thin armour-plate added – of the type used by Lawrence of Arabia. Compared to the enemy's vehicles, they were like sardine-cans, and about as easily opened. Another eight of them existed, but they were on detachment a thousand miles away, somewhere in the Western Desert. RAF Habbaniya lay under threat in no uncertain manner.

Against the ground troops we could muster the 400 British soldiers with their officers of the KORR from India, who had rifles and some trench-mortars. The rest of our ground-force consisted of 6 companies – 1,000 strong all told – of locally-enlisted Iraqis. Admittedly they were from Assyrian tribes and, as we knew, they hated other Iraqis more than they hated us, but – if it came to an armed conflict – would they prefer to shoot their blood-brothers, or us? We could only keep our fingers crossed, and hope they made the choice in our favour.

The two unassailable, and contradictory, facts for Smart were that the growing enemy army surrounding him was clearly a military matter but, as they came from an allied country with whom we had a Treaty of mutual support, it was equally clearly political. What *was* he to do?

At 6 a.m. an Iraqi officer reported at the main gate, bearing a white flag, with a message from the CO of the Iraqi troops on the plateau. He was taken to Smart, in his office, where he produced the following letter:

For the purpose of training we have occupied the Habbaniya hills. Please make no flying or the going out of any force or persons from the cantonment. If any aircraft or armoured car attempts to go out it will be shelled by our batteries, and we will not be responsible for it.

Live shelling? From troops on a *training exercise*? It was both curious, and unsettling.

At this Smart gave the Iraqi courier a letter and sent him back, with his white flag, to the enemy CO. It said:

Any interference with training flights will be considered an 'act of war' and will be met by immediate counter-offensive action. We demand the withdrawal of the Iraqi forces from positions which are clearly hostile and must place my camp at their mercy.

He received neither reply, nor reaction, and the build-up of enemy forces continued apace.

Smart's pre-breakfast reaction was to take a great big retrograde step. He went right back to First World War Army thinking. He gave orders to commandeer all the airmen, all the pupils and junior officers – excepting only his own staff and the instructors – requiring them to drop everything and – under the guidance of our army personnel – start digging First World War-style trenches for defence, and to man machine-gun posts around the camp. We squealed to the Butcher. We argued that if the Iraqis were to start something, Smart's trenches and machine-guns could not possibly stop a tank, whereas a determined effort from the air, with all we could fly from the School's armed machines, might hold the rebels at bay. Our cries to him fell on deaf ears. The AVM had issued his orders and 'orders are to be obeyed' he said.

As Smart would not countenance giving us back our ground-crews from the trenches and machine-guns, it was left to the School's pilots to move and arm the aircraft alone, during the day, in sweltering temperatures of above 100 degrees. First and foremost, wherever possible, we dispersed our machines behind hangars and trees, out of sight of the enemy guns.

Meanwhile, as far as could be done without ground-staff, the School began the shift to a pre-planned war-posture. The bane of our superiors during April had been our non-training diversions – such as arming our aircraft – to be better prepared for an emergency. Now, although we had been badly caught out by events, the diversions paid off. Praises be, we also got thirty-six hours grace before the balloon finally went up.

All the available aircraft were divided into three so-called 'Squadrons'. First, the Audaxes – to work as two bomber squadrons under the overall command of Wing Commander Larry Ling. The first squadron, the twelve machines with two 250lb bombs each, would be run by Wing Commander John Hawtrey. The second squadron, the nine Audaxes carrying eight 20lb-bombs each, would be headed by Wing Commander Selyn-Roberts. Selyn-Roberts was really an engineer, but he wore pilot's wings and we roped him in. These two last-named wing commanders were from the three whom we had managed to cull from Headquarters. The third wing commander from that source was Paul Holder. His name is not recorded in any official history but he was given a roving commission, to fly Audaxes for anybody. All the Audaxes would operate from the polo-pitch. Four wing commanders operating twenty-one Audaxes from out-of-sight of the enemy sounded a bit pushy to me but who was I, a mere Squadron Leader, to argue?

The remaining aircraft, no less than forty-three of them, were of three different types with two separate tasks – fighters and bombers. All had been lumped together as a further 'squadron', to be run by me, in plain view of our enemy, from the main airfield. Being one of the scarce pilots, there was no way I could command and control them all together, and fly full-time. Delegation of command was essential. So I split them, to operate as three separate flights under my overall direction.

My largest 'flight' would be the twenty-seven Oxfords as bombers, which I would run myself. Also, being the only pilot with any photographic-survey experience, photographing would all come to me. The second 'flight' would be the nine Gladiator fighters under Flight Lieutenant Dicky Cleaver – hopefully defending us from the more modern and numerous Iraqi Air Force – if they turned up. Lastly the seven Gordon bombers under Flight Lieutenant David 'Horse' Evans. He suffered his nickname, Horse, quite happily because he had been a jockey before the war and was still mad about riding. All my forty-three assorted machines could only operate from the main airfield, because there was no more room on the polo-pitch. The main airfield provided a perfect field-of-fire under the noses of the Iraqi gunners, machine-gunners and riflemen. Thank you very much! It was not encouraging.

Our crucial shortage was pilots. We searched as deeply as we could. Not one single pilot we had, or found, could properly be classed as both operationally experienced *and* medically fit for ops. Most were instructors, keen as mustard but who, through no choice of their own, had never fired a bullet or dropped a live bomb in anger. Some were pilots who, for varying reasons, had been put on the shelf as 'unsuitable for operational flying'. One, entitled to wings, had promptly detached himself and driven in from our Embassy in Baghdad. Some had been filched from the Headquarters Staff but they were woefully short of productive flying-training, or recent practice. Some yellow-livered staff officers had pleaded age or some dubious infirmity, claiming they were unable to take part. There were three pilots, sent to the School specifically for a 'rest' after a surfeit of operational sorties; one Warrant Officer, one Flying Officer, and me. No one had imagined what sort of 'rest' we would be getting.

We finally managed to earmark, from all that lot put together, thirty-seven qualified pilots who could – and would – fly. The twenty-one Audaxes were to get eighteen pilots; My forty-three machines would have nineteen. This, with Larry Ling and me, made thirty-nine all told to take the air.

The aircrew situation was worse. There were the two experienced bomb-aimers and four part-time rear-gunners, whom we had been using to pass on their skills to the pupils. Larry took one bomb-aimer with two gunners, and so did I. It was faintly possible, but highly unlikely that we could let part-trained pupils try to operate from the main airfield under the noses of the enemy guns, or from a minuscule polo-pitch surrounded by trees – keen and brave as they might be. So we set about hijacking pupils, ground-crew volunteers, and any other odd-bods we might find and co-opt, in an effort to fill the vacant seats of missing aircrew members.

A motley, untrained fighting force of thirty-nine aeroplanes! We knew full well that the Iraqis had a substantial and more modern Air Force with many British-trained pilots. Their nominal strength was seven squadrons. They had over seventy operational aircraft – with crews. They had Italian Savoia bombers and Breda fighters. They had American Northrop fighters. All those were fast, modern monoplanes. They had Audaxes with more powerful engines than ours. Would that formidable force join in, more numerous and better armed? And in what manner? And how could we counter it with our obsolete and slower biplanes?

Butcher created a small operations room in one of the offices, very sensibly at the back of the hangar, furthest away from the guns on the plateau. He sent me off early in the morning to make discreetly the first of several sets of pictures of the plateau. Photo-mosaic maps, made from these, showed the dispositions of the enemy. From the first mosaic, we could see that their build-up progressed alarmingly.

At last Smart had his internal preparations under way. There was the trench digging. The School was being reshaped for possible ops. The pilots were re-parking the aircraft. Now he turned his attention outside the camp. First, a report by signal to the Ambassador (Kinahan Cornwallis) in Baghdad, to Basrah, to Middle East, to India, and to London, telling them about his written exchanges with the Iraqi envoy. He also asked the Ambassador to get the continually increasing Iraqi forces withdrawn immediately, as the danger might compel him to take air action.

At what should have been breakfast time he sent another signal to the same comprehensive list of addressees, telling of the continuing build-up of troops and fighting vehicles – and adding the unwelcome news that guns and howitzers were now trained on the camp. He forecast that he might have to take air-action later in the day – to pre-empt an enemy night attack which he could not repulse. Lastly, he pleaded for air-reinforcements, on that very day.

By mid-morning Cornwallis had replied, saying that Smart's parley with the Iraqi envoy was fine, but not to take air-action before the Foreign Office in London had said its piece and given permission.

At about 11.30 the Iraqi envoy was back again. This time he said that as the British had broken the terms of the 1930 Treaty, the Iraqi CO could not allow training or anything else to be done, and this would continue for as long as the terms of the Treaty were not respected. Before answering, Reggie and his staff took some time off to think about that one.

Smart's thoughts at this stage of the proceedings are also on record. Poor man, he lacked any official Directive as to what would be right and proper in such a situation. The existing fronts in Libya and Greece made it unlikely that any reinforcements for Iraq could be spared. The fact that Iraq was supposedly our ally made it a political matter. It was quite logical therefore, he thought, that higher authority would *prefer* him to accede to the immediate Iraqi demands and leave the politicians to sort it out by negotiation – rather than risk opening up yet another campaign. You may remember that up to that time this had been the, regretted, choice of General Wavell and Air Marshal Longmore in Cairo. However, Longmore had now been replaced by Air Marshal Tedder, who was still an unknown quantity.

Any ground-attack by us, with no guns or armour, was totally out of the question. On top of that the camp had no defensive strength, or defensive works worth a row of beans. The build-up of enemy forces was proceeding fast; every passing hour therefore decreased our chances of success if we were to try and drive away the investing force by air-attack. These were good grounds for taking air-action as soon as possible on the clear choice that, with surprise, 'attack is the best form of defence.' Also, any Iraqi attack after dark would completely nullify our only counter-weapons – the School's hastily modified training aircraft.

On the other hand, what if an Iraqi counter-attack on land was made in reply to our air-strike? There was no artillery to shoot back. What was the reliability of our Assyrian-Iraqis? There were the 250 women and children from Baghdad to be considered; they had come mainly in RAF trucks while Paul Holder, flying an Oxford fitted with wireless, kept in touch with Habbaniya and watched over the convoy from above. Air evacuation to Basrah had been started at once, but they could not possibly all be gone by that evening. Lastly, and far from least, there were 9,000 civilians in the camp, mostly locally engaged Iraqis whose reactions – ranging from running away to active sabotage – were totally impossible to forecast. And for them he only had 4 days' rations.

Taken all round, Smart could see that there were many powerful arguments for making an air-attack as soon as possible before things got any worse. Conversely, there were many equally powerful reasons for *not* making an attack. It is officially recorded that he finally came to the conclusion that with no guidance from above, and in line with the earlier policy of negotiation and avoiding a flare-up, he had better do nothing.

His decision to sit tight and take no action was very sound, for a totally different and overriding reason. There was no possible way of making any air attack. Smart had destroyed any chance of getting a loaded aircraft into the air by removing all the technicians, armourers, mechanics, NCO's, the pupils, and any other essential warm bodies. They were scattered here and there about the camp while they dug trenches and then manned them with rifles and machine-guns. They had been quickly spread around by various army officers on the spot, to work in whichever places they had selected. Nobody, but nobody, knew where named individuals had been placed, so key people could not have been found and recalled, however vitally they were needed.

With the best will in the world, there was no earthly way in practice that the pilots by themselves could have fuelled and serviced the machines, found bombs and ammunition, loaded them, been briefed and, finally, started the aircraft. In those days, in addition to the man in the cockpit to operate the switches, throttle and brakes, a second person had to wind a starting-handle to get the engine going, Therefore any air-action, direct or counter-offensive, would have been completely impossible.

That gem of order and disorder is duly documented, but not in the RAF official history.

Next, believe it or not, to our horror Smart personally required Larry to take an Audax in the late morning and make a provocative flight, in order to have the Iraqis take the initiative and start something – in line with their threats. Thank Heavens, they didn't.

About midday, Smart sent a delightfully weasel-worded message back to the Iraqi commander. He said that the terms of the 1930 Treaty were a political matter, so it was being passed to the Ambassador. Meanwhile, would he kindly withdraw his forces?

He then despatched another multiple-address signal to anyone who might be concerned, giving the gist of the second message and his reply. He concluded by saying that his inaction was in accord with previous policy – as he saw it – but added, not unreasonably, *please* could he have an immediate Directive on what he ought to do – and what about sending him some reinforcements?

Soon, a third message came from the Iraqi CO. It said that they would do nothing hostile, if Habbaniya did not do so. However, they could not leave without orders from Baghdad. Smart must have given a deep sigh of relief. He had some more breathing space. Smart's reply acknowledged the message and warned the Iraqis to keep well clear of the camp during darkness to avoid any unpleasant incident.

Next, the Ambassador came on the scene with his penny worth. His signal said that he personally was all for air attack at once as the Iraqi threats constituted Acts of War. While he waited for the Foreign Office in London to decide, he was still trying to get the Iraqis to pull out. This was of little practical help to Smart.

A whole series of signals then flashed back and forth during the afternoon, evening and night.

Smart asked the Ambassador for directions on issuing an ultimatum to the Iraqis, or on making an air attack at once. The reply did nothing to help; it said that while prompt action would have been best, London's answer must be awaited. Nevertheless, the Ambassador sympathised with Smart's dilemma.

Air Marshal Tedder in Cairo promised that ten Wellington heavy bombers would be sent to Basrah and, if the Ambassador agreed, they should be used immediately *if the Iraqs opened fire!* This was an equally impractical instruction; if the Iraqis made any attack on the camp, the Wellingtons from Basrah 300 miles away could have no chance of arriving overhead in less than three to five hours – by which time the camp would assuredly have been overrun, for we had no counter whatever to any attack by Iraqi armour.

The Iraqi troop concentration continued to build up during the day.

1 May 1941

After midnight on the 1st, four messages of moral support came, but no firm Directive. One was from the Ambassador, saying that he would back anything that Smart decided to do. The second was from the Commander In Chief India (Habbaniya was still part of India Command) who said that in his judgement Smart should attack the Iraqis at once. The third was from the General in Basrah, saying that his forces could not help Smart (because of extensive flooding) but that Middle East should send help by air. The fourth came at breakfast-time from the Foreign Office in London, saying that the situation had to be cleared up; Smart was free to make any decisions himself, on the spot, including air action.

These messages all added up to extensive sympathy but no direct instructions. Smart wriggled. He believed, or at least he hoped, an ultimatum would be effective. He thought it worth trying. However he saw little sense in issuing it to the local commander who would have to refer it upwards to his High Command in Baghdad. Further, a time limit of three clear hours would have to be allowed before any signs of withdrawal from the plateau could appear. Then, if an air-attack had to be started, Smart wanted to be sure of a free and complete day ahead. So, he reckoned, the best line would be to have Ambassador Cornwallis issue the ultimatum directly in Baghdad, at 5 a.m. the following morning – 2 May – thus leaving the whole day open from 8 a.m. in case the ultimatum was unsuccessful. He sent this as a request to the Ambassador and, as before, repeated it to everyone else who, hopefully, might give him any positive input.

The Ambassador nearly caused poor Smart a heart attack at lunch-time with the news that he had told London he was asking for air-action, on that very day, at once. Smart sent back a polite but firm refusal to start anything with less than half a day remaining.

Another bombshell then came from Tedder, in some ways Smart's immediate boss. It gave him two alternatives. First, to tell the Iraqis that he would continue flying training, and start doing so. Second choice was to issue an ultimatum for the Iraqis to withdraw at once. If either failed or if the Iraqis opened fire, he was to attack the Government offices in Baghdad and, if needed, the Raschid Barracks on its outskirts.

In hindsight, an attack as recommended by Tedder would have ensured certain disaster. Raschid Ali had promised the Germans free use of Habbaniya a mere two weeks previously. In his mood as we now know it, and in his belief of promised and imminent Axis support, any attack on his home base would surely have caused him to order his investing commander to send his tanks and troops straight in to Habbaniya under a barrage of shell-fire. They had about 28 field-guns and howitzers dug in, with tanks and armoured cars impervious to our rifles and machine guns. They were supported by 5,000 to 9,000 troops. An attack by his forces already in place would have been irresistible. They could have driven a tank straight up to Smart's office and poked its gun through his office window and there was nothing whatsoever he, or we, could possibly have done to stop them.

In that case, capitulation of Habbaniya to the Iraqi enemy would have followed as surely as night follows day and Raschid Ali's promise to provide the Axis with free use of all airfields in Iraq would have been fulfilled. Thereafter, our position in Iraq would have been hopeless.

Luckily, in a sense, Tedder's signal was overtaken by events. Dhibban village, just outside the camp fence, had been occupied. The besieging force had been increased; additional guns were being placed in position on the opposite side to the plateau. All the alternatives Smart had hoped for, or which had been suggested to him, had now become impractical.

Fortunately, at last he found himself supported by the solid and down-to-earth telegram he craved. It came from London, sent by the Prime Minister, Winston Churchill. It said:

If you have to strike, strike hard.

Reggie Smart came to a difficult, nerve-racking for him, and therefore courageous decision. Recognising that it might be fatal to let the Iraqis strike the first blow, he would attack at dawn the next day, without warning, using everything he had.

His attack, exclusively from the air, would be against ground forces. Success from the air alone against well dug-in armoured troops would be most unlikely – it had never been achieved in warfare before. If it failed, he would be blamed for removing any chance of a negotiated settlement. If it succeeded, he could be taken to task for making an attack on a hitherto friendly nation when it might have been negotiated. Either way, he would be the loser.

When the chips are down, the man at the top and on the spot – in both senses – knows it all depends on him. It is described as 'the loneliness of command.' Smart must have felt himself far out on a limb and very, *very* lonely.

He told the Butcher to have his Squadron Commanders ready for a conference he, Smart, would hold at 8 p.m. that evening. At the conference he told us that if the Iraqis were still on the plateau at dawn next morning, 5 a.m., a bombing and ground-strafing attack would be started. We also learned that ten Wellington bombers of 70 Squadron had arrived at Basrah, and would be joining in from there. This was great news. 70 Squadron was, I knew, commanded by an old friend of mine, Wing Commander Tommy Rivett-Carnac, DSO, DFC. We were trained together. He was a very brave man, earning his decorations for gallantry in Bomber Command. It seemed like a good omen.

We brought up sundry practical problems, such as lack of facilities for prompt supply of bombs, fuel supplies for the polo-pitch which up to then had only been used as an overnight aircraft-parking space, and so forth. These were all brushed aside with: 'Concentrated bombing, without warning, will be very demoralising for them. It won't last long. They should be in full flight within about three hours. Do the best you can. Have every aircraft in the air before light, and start bombing as soon as you can distinguish targets on the ground – 5 a.m.'

He still flatly refused to let any of the ground crew and pupils leave their trenches round the camp, insisting that they were essential as the only defence of the camp against an attack by night – the only defence.

So – the brief was simple. Continuous bombardment and strafing with as many aircraft as practicable until they had gone. The squadron commanders went back to their squadrons.

Then – and for goodness' sake keep it quiet from Headquarters – all the squadron CO's went round the perimeter of the camp, searching out and spiriting away all the ground-crews and the pupils, leaving it completely bare. Then we allocated their tasks and named the aircrews for the next day. None of us got away to our rooms before midnight, and the last man was back at his aircraft by 0315.

The instructors found it all to be wildly exciting. Every single one of them knew an anonymous and sorrowful little poem which was pinned up in flight offices of flying schools everywhere. Habbaniya was no exception. It is called 'The Flying Instructor's Lament'. There are many versions, and it grew ever longer as embryo poets composed more and more verses to suit the circumstances of the moment. These few stanzas will suffice:

> What did you do in the War, Daddy?
> How did you help us to win?
> Circuits and bumps, and turns, Laddie,
> And how to get out of a spin.

> Alack-and-a-day, and misery me,
> As I trundle around in the sky;
> Instead of machine-gunning Nazis
> I am teaching young hopefuls to fly.

> Thus is my Service rewarded –
> My years of experience paid.
> Never a Hun have I followed down,
> Nor ever gone out on raid.

> And as soon as you've finished with one Course,
> Like a flash up another one bobs,
> And there's four more to show round the cockpit,
> And four more to try out the knobs.
>
> So it's circuits and bumps from morning to noon,
> And instrument flying till tea.
> Hold her off, give her bank, put her undercart down.
> You're slipping – you're skidding – that's me!

Those young mentors in the art of flying hugged themselves ecstatically at the thought of the challenge facing them, and what they might be able to do next morning – and regretting it was scheduled to last only three hours. Others, with some operational experience, were not quite so sanguine, nor so enthusiastic.

Philip Guedalla in his book *The Middle East* writes: 'The significance of the situation was not missed by one qualified observer. One evening, just about this time, a Messerschmitt landed in Renfrewshire; and when Rudolph Hess announced the terms on which his Führer was prepared to stop the war, the sole requirement outside Europe (apart from something about the German colonies) was that the British should evacuate Iraq.'

Eight
The Battle: Day 1

Any hopes of using some part-trained pupils as pilots had, naturally, gone clean out of the window. A night take-off – *and* with an enemy less than one mile away – demanded a kind of flying far beyond their competence. But every other pilot we had collected was there and ready to fight – all thirty-nine of us. As soon as the first signs of a grey sheen showed across the eastern night sky we started our engines. This, as any old Middle Eastern hand can tell you, is thirty minutes before you can distinguish objects on the ground from above. Those on the polo-pitch had been guided into position with torches and pointed in the right direction. Then, open the throttle and burst up into the air like a startled sparrow so as to be sure of missing the casuarina and pepper trees at the far end of the take-off run. Soon, we of the airfield contingent, guided by the hooded torches, sneaked out of the gates one by one. And, pointing our noses to the right of where the plateau had to be, opened the throttles to be up and out away from the enemy on the ground as fast as we could make it. No flare-path or navigation lights for anybody, of course.

The Iraqis, having insisted that we should not fly, under penalty of being shelled if we did so, must have wondered what in hell was going on.

As the daylight got stronger we could see that the air above the plateau was like the front of a wasps nest on a sunny morning. The ten Wellingtons were there from Basrah making a total of forty-nine aircraft of five different types and speeds, clustering and jockeying over an area not much bigger than a minor golf course. It was a hairy experience. In my Oxford I would peer down into the dusk, trying to distinguish a juicy target like a gun-emplacement – and an Audax would swoop past at some crazy angle. Or a Wellington would sail majestically across my bows, giving me heart failure and leaving my machine bucketing about in its slipstream. Luckily, no one hit anybody else, but there were some very close shaves indeed.

My experienced observer/bomb-aimer in the Oxfords was Sergeant Arthur Prickett. He was sandy-haired, of medium height, a former Halton apprentice aged thirty-one. He was six years older than I was, and to me he became a tower of strength. He had brought along a young trainee, named White, to be our rear-gunner. Prickett's bombing corrections were impeccable, and he had an eye like a hawk when it came to picking out pom-pom guns, machine-gun emplacements or other unpleasant devices.

Dead on five o'clock our first bombs went down. Within moments we could see the flashes of guns on the plateau, shelling the camp fiercely, and corresponding flashes in the camp as the shells burst. However, as the flashes on the plateau gave away the gun-positions – we retaliated. The Wellingtons seemed to be very precise with the multiple machine-guns in their front and rear power-operated turrets. The Iraqi pom-poms were using a lot of tracer, luckily, which marked them very clearly so we could try and keep out of their way.

Chief Technician Tom Brown now lives in Norfolk. He was an airman working as a target-packer and winch-operator with the Gordon flight. He told me the story of how he had volunteered early-on for what he thought would be a 'bit of fun'; something to look forward to, flying as a temporary air-gunner in a Gordon. Shaking his head at the memory, he said: 'My first run over the plateau soon wiped the smile from my face. I well remember speaking to my pilot through the Gosport speaking-tubes and asking what were the coloured lights which seemed to float gently up from below, then zip past and disappear above. When he answered, tersely, "That's tracer", my mouth suddenly became quite dry. I was instantly aware that the wooden floor and doped fabric no longer gave me the protective shell which I was used to, sitting or standing in for hours, when on the tow-line during air-to-air practice-gunnery.'

Tom Brown was far from being the only man with a dry mouth over the plateau.

Although shells were falling all over the camp, the Iraqi gunners never targeted the hospital – which had a large red-cross on its roof. The aircraft on the polo-pitch were comparatively fortunate. The line of trees hid their landing and parking areas and they could actually get their wheels off the ground before the enemy gunners caught sight of them. My three flights, Gordons, Gladiators and Oxfords, were horribly exposed at the edge of the airfield and not so lucky. Take-offs and landings on the airfield, after daylight spread, had to be made in plain view of the gunners.

There is a vulgar air force expression which is 'split-arse'. It has the meanings 'clever-clever' and 'risk-taking'. Hair-raising might be a more couth term. Being 'split' is normally a punishable offence. Now, our lives depended on it.

In an Oxford, it went something like this. After completing the cockpit checks in the shelter of the hangars I looked to an airman, positioned to one side and hidden from the plateau, but who could see the airfield. He would give the all clear if another machine was not on its way in and about to scoot round the corner of the hangars, back into comparative safety. Juggling with throttles and brakes, the machine would be made to sweep out, into view of the enemy guns, engines flat out, squirting through the open gate in the camp fence and already doing 30mph before we even reached the airfield's edge. The instant I had just enough flying speed, drag her off the ground, drop a wing and pull her round, away from the plateau in the steepest turn I dared to make. Then, take a deep breath, throttle back a little bit, retract the wheels (only in an Oxford of course; no one else had retractable wheels) and pile on height before seeking out the targets. We then bombed from 1,000 feet for maximum accuracy. Landing was an equally crazy bunch of hazards, based wholly on the sentiment 'what is the *least* dangerous thing to do?'

The Audaxes had a different set of problems. Getting off was comparatively simple.

They could start up and line up for take-off out of sight of the enemy. They came into view when they were already well on their way. Landing was not so easy. The polo-pitch/golf-course space was relatively small. Most of the pilots motored in, below tree-top height, just above the Euphrates river; this path took them along the opposite side to the airfield and away from the Iraqi-occupied plateau beyond it. Then, at a precise point, they could lift up a few feet to clear the trees and swing round in a tight turn to finish just short of, and pointing at, the landing-area; cut the power, swish-tail hard to lose surplus speed – and make a neat landing.

Our lot had different problems, at least so far as the less-agile Gordons and Oxfords were concerned. I devised and used an approach to the main airfield that could, at best, be classed as bizarre. As soon as Prickett called 'Last bomb gone!', my solution was to swing the aircraft away from the plateau's machine-guns and pom-poms, and disappear, over the river, on the far side of the camp. From there, sneak in very low down indeed, seeking and getting the best cover possible from buildings and trees alongside the roads. Turn in between the hangars – to frustrate the pom-poms – and bank smartly right to land on the taxi-strip beside the airfield fence. Brake hard – and swing in through the gate still doing about 20mph and, swish round behind the hangars again – and stop. My first approach turned out reasonably well and I had not been hit. It promptly became the pattern for all my pilots working off the airfield under shell-fire.

Naturally, the Iraqis soon came round to the other side of the river, taking pot-shots with rifles and machine-guns at the aircraft flying past them, low and slow over the water, about fifty yards from their noses. Our army promptly set up rifles and machine guns on our side of the river. Very soon, any Iraqi opposite found it most unhealthy to try and draw a bead on an aircraft. So they left again.

We, the aircrew, were only too well aware that we had nothing, just nothing, which could stop a tank driving up to the front door of AHQ – except our bombs. Hence we knew our very survival depended on, in effect, knocking out every offensive weapon or vehicle before the Iraqis could pull themselves together and bring it to bear effectively. And to keep on, and on, without respite till they left – which thank goodness should be within hours, as Smart had confidently told us. This drove us into a routine which was to fly, fly, fly in any offensive aircraft we could get our hands on. We bombed, and gunned, and looked for other targets. Something had to crack, and it could not be us.

As soon as any aircraft was back on the ground, one of the two crew-members – we took turns alternately – would report to the Butcher in his ops room, telling him the results and also suggesting suitable new targets which had been spotted during a sortie. Butcher would then plot both bits of information on the latest photo-map that I had produced for him, and allot the crewman his next target. While that was going on the other crewman – pilot, or pupil acting as bomb-aimer – would help reload the machine and make a quick check for any additional damage which was worse than superficial. 'Superficial' meant any new hole (where a bullet or piece of shrapnel had gone through) which did not appear to have damaged something important – like a main-spar, an oil pipe, or a control-hinge. Usually, this would all be done with the engines still running. Surprisingly, no one got clouted by a spinning prop. When the first chap came back from the ops room with the new targets, off they went again.

After their crash-courses the pupils, acting as bomb-aimers and rear-gunners, quickly became remarkably accurate – even if some of the bombing-run corrections were a bit garbled at first. Not like Prickett's placid and experienced – 'Left, left…Steady…Right…Steady…' and ending up with a flat 'Bombs gone' – which I was hearing as the tracers flicked by. More like, to begin with: 'Left, left…Right…Right…RIGHT…LEFT, LEFT!!! Oh Christ, bombs gone…Sir.' However, they all did a fabulous, dangerous and courageous job. And soon they became highly proficient.

Ground-fire was both intense and accurate. Over the plateau, the Oxfords were cruising at about 1,000 ft. One would fly steadily on a bombing-run (as was essential with those old-fashioned bomb-sights), sitting and watching bullet-holes being punched up through the wings from underneath. Most aircraft received several bullet strikes through the cockpit itself. The dive-bombing and machine-gunning Audaxes went far lower than we did. Every machine was damaged to some extent but the record went to an Audax flown by Flight Lieutenant Dan Cremin. He brought his aircraft back from a single ten-minute sortie with fifty-two new bullet holes in it. Miraculously, he had no bullet-holes through his person, but his pupil-gunner was less fortunate. He was carted off to hospital, seriously wounded.

For man or machine the rule was the same: minor damage, or minor wounds that were not incapacitating, keep cracking. No respite – no breaks. Anyone who had no more than a flesh wound returned to the attack as fast as the planes could be re-armed and re-crewed. The terms 'minor-damage', or 'flesh-wounds' might have been stretched a bit and not assessed in a normal RAF manner – but then our situation was far from normal.

In the Gordon Flight there was a rear gunner called 'Wad' Taylor. How he collected that nickname is uncertain, but it was probably because he always took what the Scots call a 'piece' into the air with him – a thick sandwich of bread and butter. And, in the Services, since time immemorial, a slice of bread has always been a Wad. From our Indian Empire days comes 'char and a wad' – tea with bread-and-butter. Anyway, Taylor was taking chomps at his wad, between his bursts of Lewis-gun fire, when he suddenly felt as though someone had hit him on the forehead with a hammer. He shook his head and put up his hand. He could feel warm liquid trickling down into his right eye and, with the other one he could see his fingers covered in blood. 'Good God!' he thought, 'it's *my* blood!' He chose not to tell his pilot, because he thought he would be too busy to want, or need, to know. He just shut his bad eye and, using the good one, carried on firing. His forehead soon began to throb.

Sorties did not last long. It was get airborne, up over the targets, drop the bombs and back down again. So it was but a few minutes later that his Gordon was back behind the hangars once more, away from the enemy guns. An enemy bullet had come up through the plywood floor and grazed his cheek. Next, it sliced up through his right eyebrow. Then it had passed inside the front of his leather flying helmet, cutting a deep furrow through the flesh of his forehead on the way. Finally, it left through the top of his helmet. We packed him off to hospital and luckily, apart from aches and pains, he was not badly hurt. Above all, he could work. Stitched, bandaged and plastered, his head looked like a white pumpkin, but he was back on flying within an hour or two and, from then on, he never missed a day. The scar above his right eye made a permanent reminder of a 'very close call'. He assuredly earned the Distinguished Flying Medal which was awarded to him some time later.

Our graver casualties were, however, mounting alarmingly. Those who came back seriously wounded were displaying a rare mixture of courage and skill. Flight Lieutenant Jimmy Broughton, an Audax pilot, was shot through the jaw, with the bullet lodging in his face and causing great pain. He could barely see, but even so he managed to land, on the polo-pitch, in one piece. Another was shot through the thigh with the bullet splitting in two; one piece lodged half way between knee and groin and the other tracked up to his rump, but he got the aircraft back without a crash. Another Audax pilot had three bullets through his right lung and shoulder, causing him to collapse over the stick and push it forwards. The machine began to plunge earthwards. The pupil crew-member behind him realised that – to put it mildly – things were far from normal in the driver's seat. Although he also had been wounded, he managed to reach over to the front cockpit and, perilously near the ground, succeeded in pulling the pilot back into an upright position, and hold him there. He, though only half conscious and with only the use of his left hand, managed to pull the aircraft out of its dive, bring it back, and land it on the polo-pitch – before he passed out cold. The doctors in the hospital forecast that his injuries would probably be fatal but, luckily, they were proved wrong; he pulled through eventually.

Some did not get back at all. One of my Oxfords was shot down in flames; the instructor, Flying Officer Gillespy was killed, together with two of our pupil-crewmen.

Tom Brown tells of another experience: 'I was crew to a Gordon pilot who was shot in the back of his thigh when we were hit by a burst of ground-fire. Although in great pain he managed to land her okay. The machine had also been hit in the oil-cooler and lost all its oil pressure. We just had enough lubrication left to taxi almost to the wheeled gates in the airfield's fence, which we were aiming to enter, when the oil-less engine seized-up solid. We ran, or rather he hobbled with my assistance, to the safety of the space behind the hangars. Quite soon afterwards I watched the old Gordon first being bracketed by shell-fire and then suffer a direct hit which saw her off in the usual flames and black smoke.'

We began with four wing commanders all told; three from the Headquarters, and Larry Ling. I had envied them because, being more senior than I was, they seemed to have 'happened' to get the 'fun-job' – if any of it could be called fun. They were doing all the dive-bombing in the normally docile Audaxes. More; being on the polo-pitch, they were out of sight of the enemy between flights. It seemed they had had all the luck. However, it was not long before I came to the to the opinion that it was they who were in fact grasping the shitty end of the stick, instead of their junior – me. On that first day, of the four wing commanders:

Larry didn't last till lunch-time. Following an extremely painful and uncomfortable flight back to the polo-pitch, he was taken off by ambulance to lie on his face because of a bullet clean through his bum-muscles. No doubt he felt unfortunate, but at least he was spared the rest of the campaign.

Selyn-Roberts, running one of the squadrons, also had no lunch. He was carted off in another squealing ambulance for an emergency appendix operation.

Paul Holder was shot down. He was not hurt badly, and was able to re-start flying, after a short break to get patched up. Then he got shot down a second time. Again he survived. Unlucky to be shot down twice; lucky to be alive. Curiously, and perhaps because he didn't 'belong' to the school, the Butcher never mentioned him in any official document. For me, as a researcher, it was a rumour until Paul confirmed it to me himself as a true story.

That left only one Audax squadron commander in working trim, Wing Commander John Hawtrey.

The Wellingtons, being so much larger, took far more punishment. Nine got back to Basrah and all nine were found to be unserviceable. Without being in the least unfair, Basrah was not actually being shelled and they might have been able to afford normal RAF 'unserviceable' standards. Our criterion was less stringent. It would be summed up as: 'Can it get up into the air? Yes? Then off we go!'

The tenth Wellington was less fortunate. Even before its bombs had been dropped, it suffered serious damage to the engines. The pilot made a good forced landing, on the airfield. The Iraqis immediately swung their guns away from the camp as the crew piled out and sprinted for the hangars. Machine-gun bullets were kicking up the sand around them but they got there safely. Meanwhile we did our best to save the aircraft itself.

Naturally, we had no proper equipment, such as a proper Wellington-tow-bar, but within minutes a tractor was on its way out with a rope. It had an RAF armoured-car on each side, trying to screen the completely exposed driver from the enemy machine-gun and rifle bullets. By the time they reached the Wellington the firing was intense. With bullets zipping all about him, the brave tractor-driver managed to get his rope round the tail-wheel but, before he could get the aircraft under tow, the Iraqis had successfully bracketed the Wellington and scored a direct hit. It burst into flames.

By some miracle, although the shell-burst had wrecked the Wellington and had also put the tractor out of action, the tractor-driver was unhurt although he was a bit deaf from the explosion. Abandoning the burning wrecks, the commander of one of the armoured cars, Corporal Stimpson together with his crewman Aircraftman Bethel, bundled him into their car, named 'Intrepid' and then headed lickety-split for home and comparative safety. When they were about half way across the airfield, the bombs in the burning Wellington exploded, blowing it and the tractor to bits. A very gallant effort which deserved a better result.

The burnt-out carcass had to stay where it was, in the middle of the airfield, for there was no means of clearing it away under the muzzles of enemy guns.

Damage in the air was not the only cause of losing our aircraft. We did our best to hide the machines from the sight of enemy gunners on the plateau. Obviously, we couldn't put them *inside* the hangars; a fire there, with tanks full of petrol in wood-and-fabric aeroplanes, would have meant a total burn-out after the first shell came through the roof. So we tucked as many machines as we could *behind* the hangars; this provided the best measure of protection we could give because the corrugated-iron walls and roofs caught and exploded most of the shells on their way in. I'll warrant that the bangs made the Butcher's ears sing a bit, as he worked in his little office-ops-room under the hangar walls.

In spite of our efforts, another Gordon got a direct hit and blew up, killing one man and injuring two more. Two Oxfords were hit and set on fire; the lads could only pull them out of the way and let them burn.

Every pilot we had, myself included, was flying sortie after sortie as fast as the aircraft could be re-armed. At the same time, I was trying to do some kind of briefing and aircraft allocation in between. I was very tired and therefore getting very testy. I had given one of my pilots the objective of trying to silence a couple of Iraqi guns which Prickett had identified, and I had told him which Oxford to use. He padded off with his pupil bomb-aimer and it seemed only moments before he was back. 'What the blazes d'you want now?' I snapped, 'Wasn't I clear enough?' With a completely dead-pan face he just said, 'The Oxford that you just allocated to me, Sir, is on fire. Which other one should I take?'

We employed some locally recruited Iraqis as cooks, kitchen staff and barmen; they loyally remained on duty throughout. The Mess Sergeant, and the revolver which never left his hand, coupled with his series of judicious threats, could have had something to do with it. Even so, they very nearly escaped when one of the cooks sheltering behind a wall was hit by a shell splinter. Revolver in one hand and receiver in the other, the Sergeant was telephoning the hospital for an ambulance; the doc asked the fatuous question 'Are you being shelled?' What in blazes did he think? Everyone, except those in the hospital, was being shelled more-or-less continuously. The Sergeant, far from giving the type of reply which by then I or anyone else would have screamed back at him, merely said, 'Listen,' – and held the receiver outside the door. Obligingly, a shell landed. 'Good God!' floated down the line, and an ambulance was promptly despatched.

Meanwhile, Northrops, Bredas, Savoias, Audaxes and Gladiators of the numerically stronger and more modern Iraqi Air Force made sporadic attacks on the camp, mostly diving down at their highest possible speed, across and away. We had our own Gladiators on patrol which made darts at them but, having no radio or radar control, they could never catch them. Fortunately, at this early stage, the Iraqi attacks played only a minor role. They dropped some bombs pretty inaccurately, and did some strafing mainly of nuisance value – although they burned an aircraft or two from time to time.

The only bombers which did not come in low were the twin-engined Savoias. They had oxygen; we had none at Habbaniya. So they came across far higher than our Gladiator pilots could reach. One of them came over very high up indeed, making one run only, and he dropped no bombs. We presumed he must be taking photographs, in order to assess how damaged we were.

Another single Savoia was unwary enough to come over a little lower. Dicky Cleaver flying the patrolling Gladiator saw him and, although he was pretty high, say 20,000ft, he reckoned he might just make it before he lost consciousness from lack of oxygen. He climbed like a demon and got right on his tail. Savoias were made largely of wood and were not very damage-resistant. Slavering at the chops in expectation, Dicky took careful aim. Absolutely certain of his kill, he pressed the firing button. All four guns jammed – almost certainly having frozen up from the cold at that altitude and our lack of anti-freeze oil. Dicky could only gnash his teeth and watch him fly away, safe and sound.

My dachshund, Frankie, upset me a lot. He was terrified by the explosions. Anyone who has had a dog – except perhaps a sporting retriever – will know just how much they suffer from a fireworks display. Patently, with so many detonations going on all round him, he could not be left loose to run around crazily in a nervous state among the aircraft. He might flee out on to the airfield in a frenzied search for me and – the British are mad when it comes to dogs – somebody might even go out and attempt a brave rescue act. Nor did it seem fair to tie him up, outside or in, to nearly strangle himself in fear, trying to escape. And there were bomb and shell-splinters flying about too. The best I could do was to shut him in an empty office where I hoped the bursts and bangs might be a little deadened. Then, each time I landed and went to report, I fetched him to come with me. His delight at having me close to him changed to pathetic dismay when I left him again, shut in his prison once more.

Smart's forecast of enemy departure within three hours was wildly inaccurate. Half-past noon; after seven and a half hours of unremitting attack, far from the enemy being in full flight by lunchtime there seemed to have been no change or reduction in the shelling. We carried on, regardless.

A splendid Samaritan went up to the mess around lunchtime and came back with a mountain of sandwiches which we ate gratefully 'on the hoof'. We were all feeling pretty neglected and exposed, being the Iraqis' prime target, but he also brought back with the sandwiches a story which helped us a lot. While he had been waiting, six Iraqi Gladiators strafed the camp with success, for they had burned up two or three aircraft on the polo-pitch. As they pulled up to fly away, guns still firing, several stray bullets had come through the corrugated-asbestos roof of the Officers' Mess. His graphic description of dives for any available cover by the elderly and portly officers who had avoided being with us in the fighting team, and of their well-padded and rounded backsides sticking out from under tables and chairs, was scurrilous and hilarious. This assurance that they too, in some way, were not escaping our trials and tribulations cheered us up no end.

What with one thing and another going on in Habbaniya, there were only two beings apparently unmoved by the strafing, bombing and shellfire which reverberated throughout the camp. Two storks with their little family of two babies occupied their nest on top of the Headquarters' wireless-mast apparently with complete unconcern. Later on, however, they too were to have their troubles. The two fledglings both tried to fly, but crashed on take-off. One broke a wing and, despite being rushed to the intensive-care unit at the hospital, died of its wounds. The other was eaten by a jackal.

When darkness fell we got our second and equally unproductive evening briefing at Headquarters. It was the last. Smart was not there and we did not attend another. Maybe no other was ever held. The shelling continued.

We licked our wounds and took stock. On that first day, 2 May 1941, our mixed bunch of pilots had flown 193 recorded operational sorties – an average of about 6 apiece, give or take a bit. Quite a lot never got recorded. There were some other variations. The polo-pitch chaps, being hidden from, and further from the enemy, had been able to get up, bomb and land back quicker. So they did more sorties. On the other hand, the Gordons and Oxfords off the airfield did fewer sorties because they took longer – so they spent more time under enemy fire. The prime and crucial point, however, was that our enemies, in spite of our unremitting efforts, were *still* sitting on top of the plateau. All of them. Admittedly, they were showing no signs of attacking, but equally they were showing no signs of departing.

Our losses had been devastating, if you consider that our out-and-out effort had been to no apparent effect, so far. In the fourteen hours from pre-dawn to after dusk, of our sixty-four irreplaceable aircraft we had lost twenty-two – more than a third – shot down, burned out or damaged beyond short-term repair. By all normal RAF standards, many more should have been classed as unfit for flight. The fitters and riggers were working like maniacs – in the dark with hooded torches, patching and mending every machine which could reasonably or unreasonably be coaxed into the air again. Ten of our thirty-nine pilots – over a quarter – were dead or firmly in hospital. Twenty-nine of us left, and many of those wearing bandages and plasters. And all those resources gone in *one day*! It had been quite a performance and was a far, far cry from

> 'Circuits and bumps and turns, Laddie,
> And how to get out of a spin.'

During the day, although we did not know it then, the Iraqis had entered the British Embassy in Baghdad. Politely but firmly they removed all radio transmitters and receivers, and cut off the telephones. This totally divorced them from the outside world. All we could know at Habbaniya was that their radio and telephones had gone completely silent. They had managed to secrete one small civilian receiver only, so all they could hear were the complete pie-in-the sky broadcasts by the BBC, saying for example that anti-aircraft guns had been flown in for us, and that a British Army column from Palestine had already reached the villages of Ramadi and Fallujah, close by, and were about to rescue us; this when the potential rescue column had not yet even been assembled for departure!

Being the only two squadron commanders left, John Hawtrey and I put our heads together with the Butcher. The aircraft losses had been so extensive that a different division of our resources would be more efficient. We decided that John should operate all the remaining Audaxes from the polo-pitch, lumped together as one squadron. In addition, he would take over my Gladiators, moving them from behind their shell-catching hangar to his tree-screened polo-pitch. I would keep the Oxfords, and the Gordons, continuing to operate them off the airfield. Departure of the Gladiators would help in other ways. Not only did it decrease my work load, but also I could shift the Gordons up to the space behind the hangar adjacent to mine, now vacated by the Gladiators. It would put them closer to me, and just a little further from the Iraqis across the way. Finally, it would simplify both John's and my tasks overall. We each would be piloting, and operating, only two types of aircraft.

So what next? Because they were still there, the simple and only possible answer was 'Same again tomorrow'.

By the end of our discussions it was about midnight. John and I made a tour round our aircraft, partly to encourage the airmen working on them and to show we cared, and partly to get some idea of how many we might have available in the morning. Then we crawled off to our rooms. We wanted to try and get some sleep before the pre-dawn planning and briefing. We were, both of us, very, *very* tired.

Neither of us got much sleep. The night was neither placid nor restful. The Iraqis, freed from the possibility of instant retribution from the air, tossed something over 200 shells into the camp between midnight and 3 a.m. – about one a minute. Shortly before 2 a.m. I lay awake on my bed, listening. I could hear the 'sho-sho-sho' of a spinning howitzer-shell, on its way from the plateau to the camp. It landed – crumph! I muttered to myself, 'about 200 yards away, I guess.' Pause. 'Sho-sho-sho…CRUMPH!!!' Much closer. The next explosion blew the window in, scattering shards of broken glass all over the room and on to the bed. 'The next one' I muttered to myself, 'is coming in here, through the roof.'

I hastily scrambled off the bed and crawled underneath it. There, scared out of his tiny wits, shivering and whimpering, was Frankie. Personal reactions under stress are peculiar. I said to the dog, out loud, 'You bloody cissy! You're scared!' He was probably less frightened than I was, if the truth be told, but I admit now that his abject fear helped me pull myself together. I swept him up in my arms and climbed back into the bed, with him. As all dachshunds love to do, he instantly burrowed down under the sheet and curled up at the bottom, pressed tight to my ankles and apparently content. Master was in control! 'Sucker,' I thought. Little did he know how impotent I really was.

The next shell did not come through the roof; it landed just short of the bungalow, and blew in the opposite window.

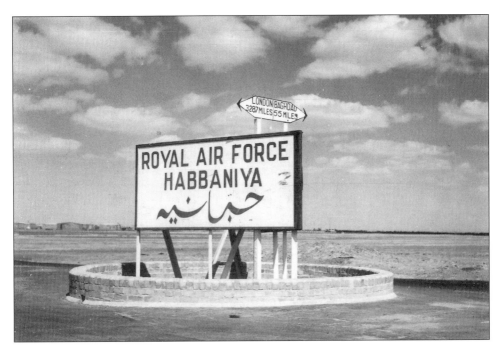

Entrance to RAF Habbaniya, Iraq

No. 4 Flying Training School, based at Habbaniya. This annual group photograph was taken in the summer before the uprising. Note the official hot weather uniform; solar topis, khaki shorts and open-necked sort-sleeved shirts. The Commanding Officer sits proudly in the middle of his men.

Reluctant aircrew officers and pupils, following AVM Smart's orders, dig defensive trenches in front of the camp buildings.

No. 4 Flying Training School Instructors before the uprising. From left to right, back row: Flt Lt Bodmin, Flt Lt Dan Cremin, Wg/Com. Larry Ling, Wg/Com. John Hawtrey, Flt Lt 'Stooge' Garner. Sitting, front, Flg Off. Kenneth Osborne-Young.

Sq Ldr Tony Dudgeon, CO 55 (Blenheim) Squadron prior to Habbaniya.

Sq Ldr Tony Dudgeon, with Frankie.

Assyrian Levies – Iraqi troops that served in the British Army and guarded Habbaniya.

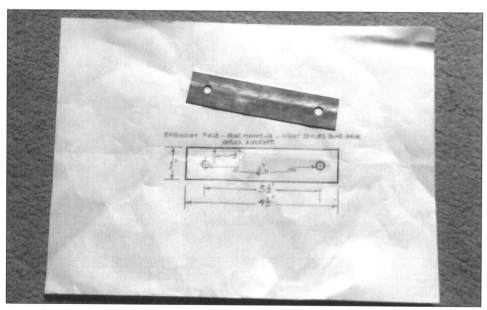

Author's drawing of his modification to the Oxford Trainer bomb-racks.

An airman checks one of the eight 20lb bombs on an Oxford aircraft for security. The tail-fins of the bombs are tilted down, projecting into the slipstream so that the bombs can be mounted on the racks in the bomb-recess.

On the first day of the Iraqi attack a damaged Wellington of No. 70 Squadron had to make a forced landing on the airfield towards the plateau in the background, on which were the Iraqi guns. A gallant attempt was made to tow the aircraft in but the Iraqi gunners found their target. Within minutes the aircraft was ablaze causing its bombs to explode.

Looking north from the polo pitch across the camp to the hangars and the airfield beyond. Strafing Iraqi Audaxes have left two aircraft burning.

Looking east. In the far background on the left, behind the row of trees, is the River Euphrates. Nearer, to the left, is the subsidiary airfield made by flattening the golf course and the polo pitch. The airfield and the enemy guns beyond it are out of sight to the far right. The trees hide the British aircraft from the guns. Nevertheless, some of them, strafed by the Iraqi Air Force, are burning fiercely. On this raid, stray bullets went through the roof of the Officers' Mess which is partly hidden by black smoke.

Sergeant Prickett double checks the bombs for security on their racks; his parachute pack is on the ground in front of the machine. On the wings two airmen are checking the level of oil in the tanks. Sergeant Prickett was killed the next day.

Airborne for a pattern-bombing raid. The No. 2 comes up alongside so that his eight 20lb bombs can be clearly seen.

73

The only photograph in existence of an Airspeed Oxford Trainer aircraft dropping a live bomb in anger. If truth be told, the inexperienced pilot was sufficiently uptight that he did not come into closer formation as his leader (the author) wished.

A few moments after taking the previous photograph, the author's machine was hit by a machine-gun bullet which entered through the perspex windscreen and went out through the roof. Fortunately it caused no serious damage.

Lorries bringing supplies to the Iraqis at night were camouflaged and concealed nearby during the day, ready for the quick run-in and away, without lights, under cover of darkness. However, our searching Audaxes could usually find and attack them.

One of the 'serviceable' Oxfords after a few days' flying. The dark patches are doped-on fabric over bullet holes. Thirty-two patches can be counted on this side view where the bullets came out of Oxford 'J'; the underneath, where the bullets went in, was no prettier.

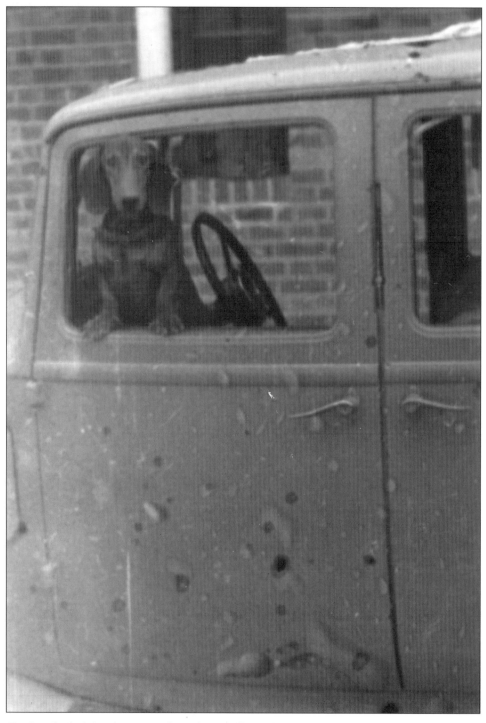

Frankie, the dachshund, waits in the author's staff car. The car was still working at this point though showing signs of wear and tear in the form of shell splinters through the side panels, roof blown off and glass all gone from the windows and screen.

An Iraqi tanker lorry found on the road from Baghdad. It has been bombed by one of the Oxfords (four small craters from 20lb bombs can be seen on the road). The fourth bomb, at about 5 yards, was close enough to set it on fire.

Two Iraqi fuel lorries, travelling from Baghdad at dawn, were found and set on fire on the road across the desert between Fallujah and Khan Nuqta.

This picture was taken before the conflict. The view, from the airfield's edge, shows bare desert and the escarpment on top of which the enemy guns were to take up position – hidden from view but firing down onto the camp.

A flight of Audaxes are lined up on the airfield, in peacetime, ready for use in training.

One of the Gladiators which in peacetime were used by Staff Officers and others as runabouts, but were, perforce, reverted to their original attack role during the conflict.

Rutbah Fort, about 200 miles west of Habbaniya on the desert route to Syria and Jordan. It was originally built as a base for protecting the oil pipeline which passed by en route from Kirkuk and Haditha to the Mediterranean.

Fallujah Bridge was an important factor in the campaign. A pontoon bridge (shown here in peacetime), it was the only means of crossing the Euphrates by road other than in Baghdad – 60 miles away. Elsewhere the river was crossed by ferryboats, none of which (if the author's memory serves) were big enough to carry a vehicle any bigger than a farm cart.

One of the RAF armoured cars. It was of First World War design, as used by Lawrence of Arabia. It consisted of a civilian Rolls Royce chassis with armour plates bolted on and heavy duty tyres. The heat inside was appalling.

Airmen survey the results of the first German raid by Heinkel 111s on the engineering and workshop hangars, 16 May.

Nine
Enemy Reactions

We cannot now know, precisely, what was in Raschid Ali's trained legal mind at the end of April 1941, but recorded facts and his actions (which were both logical and strategically sound) permit us to make some near-certain deductions. Let us review the facts.

Beyond any shadow of doubt he was extremely anti-British. It is fact that he had been plotting actively with the Germans, against us, for at least seven years. They had given him practical help, and gold, to finance his machinations. We know their grand aim was to stir up a pan-Arab holy war against the British, to which they could lend their support as the saviours of Islam. From the German archives we know, as fact, that German Foreign Affairs gave him on 8 April a written undertaking to provide financial and military aid if he got into any kind of war for freedom from the British yoke. They also record that in return he promised them, and the Italians, unrestricted use of *all* the airfields in Iraq for any military force they might send.

British archives record what he told Sir Kinahan Cornwallis the British Ambassador in Baghdad, on 23 April. He said that the British had broken the terms of the 1930 Treaty, for we had brought in an Army force and sent it on to become a part of the Habbaniya garrison, as opposed to merely staging it through the country as stated by the Treaty. Thus he held the British to have committed an Act of War against Iraq. The German records say that immediately thereafter, on 26 April, when he requested their money and military backing for a war with the British, he also advised them that his forces would be in contact with ours in a few days, and so they were. On 29 April his superior fighting force began to surround Habbaniya.

It would have been a logical and sound tactical ploy for him to delay any attack till the promised German forces were known to be on the move. Therefore, as soon as the first elements of the Iraqi force arrived, envoys were sent in to tell the British in the camp to keep very quiet, and to do nothing alarming. Further warnings were sent in later, again telling us to hold our horses. These were wholly reasonable actions, giving time both for him to build up his investing strength to a wholly overwhelming level, and also for the Germans to start their promised move.

Why Habbaniya? It was a 'soft' target with no modern defences. It was a superbly appointed camp and airfield with magnificent operational facilities, such as workshops, hangars and high-octane fuel, to name but a few. It was an ideal military installation or base between Vichy-French Syria and Baghdad. It was perfectly placed near Baghdad as the first base of a German force coming into Iraq, via their pro-Axis friends in Syria. And the nearest operational British forces to protect or re-take it were hundreds of miles away in either direction – from Egypt and Palestine, 400 miles and nothing but a vast expanse of arid desert in between. From the direction of Basrah, 300 miles distant and any ground forces they might have or obtain were cut off by floods.

Of all the Iraqi airfields – operationally, administratively, strategically and geographically it was plainly the plum gift for offering to the Germans.

No wonder he sent his force, fully armed and outwardly irresistible, to the boundaries of that camp. His force was estimated by us at the time to be 5,000 troops, with supporting guns and armour, against our 1,400 troops with neither guns nor armour – and 1,000 of those were of Iraqi nationality and therefore of uncertain value to us. Backing them was an air force with a strength of 76 fairly modern operational aircraft.

The German archives differ slightly; they record that the investing force of Iraqi soldiers numbered 9,000, and not 5,000. That extra force, if accurate, is immaterial; attack by either would have been unstoppable. Raschid Ali knew we had at Habbaniya only an extensive (and presumably non-operational) flying school. Resistance would be futile.

Following correct military practice and in order to preserve secrecy, he had an excellent cover-plan to prevent his actions being bruited around in Baghdad as hostile. Excepting only a few key personnel, the officers and men of his force had been told that they were going on a training exercise. Nevertheless, they carried large stocks of live ammunition. The Iraqi Air Force was not given any sort of 'live' knowledge; one may assume that Raschid Ali calculated they could be called into action at short notice when the balloon went up. Also, it was adroit of him to let the women and children move openly from Baghdad; their safe passage would lull everyone into an unwarranted sense of security.

It is of interest here in passing to judge the facts and see if they are commensurate with some form of local 'rebellion'[2] against us, as the Foreign Office and Whitehall treated and recorded Iraqi actions – then and long after. My researches have failed to dig out the true reason for this. I believe it to be wrapped up in some Foreign Office ploy, to re-build and preserve good relations with our political ally, Iraq (and safeguard our oil supllies). Also, for international propaganda to play down the blunt fact that we gave a long-standing ally a very bloody nose. The terms may have seemed politically convenient but 'Raschid Ali's Rebellion', 'Raschid Ali's Siege of Habbaniya' and 'Raschid Ali's Revolt', all used throughout, are not supported by logic or fact. None of Raschid Ali's moves accord in any way with a simple Iraqi 'rebellion', or 'revolt'. On the contrary, his well-documented actions add up only if accepted as moves for embarking at the beginning of May, with German support, upon a legally justifiable war aimed at liberation from all British influence in the country. And with luck, if Nasser's *coup* succeeded in Egypt, over the entire Middle East. He could have every confidence at the outset that, with promised German help, it was going to be successful. Habbaniya was stage one.

It must have looked a cinch to Raschid Ali, and one must admire his brilliant and detailed planning. All he had to do was to press the button when the Germans reacted.

---

[2] By definition, the words 'rebellion' and 'revolt', used throughout by Whitehall, refer to *civilian* uprisings and not to military affairs.

German records note that Ribbentrop, the Minister for Foreign Affairs, whose department had sent the original letter of 8 May offering help, had earlier been in favour of a powerful reaction. His plan was to send Grobba back to Iraq, tasked with causing maximum inconvenience and disruption to the British. He also advocated strong military intervention and suggested sending one full squadron of bombers and one full squadron of fighters. He asked Hitler to give the Luftwaffe the necessary instructions. He had submitted this plan to Hitler for rubber-stamping but Hitler had dragged his feet. He was wary of any serious engagement before he attacked Russia or even of having a military mission in being, working in Baghdad. The High Command (OKW) was in a grave quandary. Any kind of help would be extremely difficult, and the military command also had cold feet. Their reasons were very compelling. *Barbarossa* was on the boil and the Balkan campaign was in full flood. Iraq targets were out of range for the Luftwaffe, who had said that all they could spare would be 'a few Ju 52 aircraft for use as transports only!' At the same time (early 1941) Rommel in the Western Desert was pleading hard for reinforcements to exploit the British weakness there – caused by Wavell having lost so many tanks and troops he sent to fight in Greece. Plainly, for the German High Command to send any help at all was going to be very difficult. But, on the other hand, not to send any would entail a loss of face among the Arabs.

Perhaps the most vivid evidence showing how well Raschid Ali's cover-plan had succeeded is a verbatim quote from a letter written to me years later by Air Colonel Hofthi Aziz who had been commanding at the time an Iraqi squadron of 14 Breda-65 fighters – a fairly modern Italian-built monoplane. He wrote:

> *The main thing I wanted to say is this:*
> *Whatever happened in May 1941, we did not declare war between Habbaniya and Hinaidi…I want to know why the RAF at Habbaniya came and bombed our air force without any warning early on Friday 2 May 1941? And also they bombed our troops who were camping south of Habbaniya. This kind of thing made us mad. You know, Friday is our Sunday, and every one of us was fast asleep in his home...*

One of the principles of war is to achieve surprise, if possible. Reggie Smart achieved that in full measure. Reggie caught the troops, and Raschid Ali with their trousers down that morning.

Raschid Ali immediately got on to the German High Command, again pleading for immediate help. He also asked for the previous German envoy – Dr Grobba – to be sent back to Baghdad.

In response to Raschid Ali's pleas, Ribbentrop and Hitler together outlined on 3 May a plan for actual help that would be given to the Iraqis.

Hitler agreed straightaway to the return of Dr Grobba and a staff – but he was very reserved on the weaponry. It was obvious that military help of some kind had to be sent to Raschid Ali who was already engaged in battle, but what should that be in practical terms? Hitler came to the conclusion that only a relatively limited force would be sent and, primarily, that was in order not to lose face. Thus Hitler missed the boat, which he could have caught easily – giving him access to unlimited oil.

On 4 May they started to implement their plan. *Reichsmarschall* Göring arranged that Colonel Junck was sent for from France, and told to report to Berlin.

Ten
The Battle: Days 2-6

On the second morning, 3 May, John and I got to our squadrons at about 4 a.m. to begin briefing our crews for the 5 a.m. take-off.

There were still a few women and children in the camp, and we had to get them out, together with surplus wounded from the hospital. We had no transport aircraft and the Oxfords had no passenger seats. For the job we got help from 31 Squadron, from India, with their DC2s. The DC2 was no more warlike or damage-resistant than my Oxfords, and it was a bigger target as well as being less manoeuvrable. Their crews were indeed brave men. They arrived from Basrah at first light and we had a patrol of dive-bombing and machine-gunning Audaxes already in the air, waiting for them each day. As they hove into view the Audaxes would do their best to hammer the Iraqis to keep their heads down while the DC2s – as they had to – made their dangerous approaches over the plateau. The Audaxes did a magnificent job and only a few DC2s were damaged – none seriously. There were no passengers injured. The women and children were all gone in a day or so. There was an exception. Mrs (now Lady) Holman refused to distance herself from her husband in the Baghdad Embassy. She was married to the Councillor and Deputy to the British Ambassador – which meant that she carried enough clout to be allowed to stay. She worked with the nurses among the wounded and did not leave for Basrah until the first stage of the campaign was over.

Before all the other women had left, a spate of fascinating rumours whizzed round the hangars. Their subject – reasons why the boss had departed! The only known and incontrovertible fact was that AVM Reggie Smart had gone to Basrah in one of the returning DC2s. Smart's reputation has suffered on that account and I have done my utmost to find the truth, with only part success. Mainly it is because over fifty years have passed, and memory plays peculiar tricks. Also, the written records differ widely. Here is the best I can do.

The rumours flying around were fantastic. They began, quite simply, with the surmise that Reggie's nerve had cracked. We saw no shame in that – he was by no means the only person to have that problem. There was a bit added on, to the effect that he had been injured in some way. The first version was that he had been driving along a road at night in pitch darkness, with no lights for they would have attracted a shell from an Iraqi field-gun. His alleged reasons for driving himself went all the way from going to the hospital because of his nerves, to speeding down the road in the blackout and meeting another car head on – sending him to the hospital willy-nilly. Both appear to be quite untrue.

Another tale, reported by Paul Holder, is by far the most colourful. Having no benefit of radar or warning devices, we had installed a lookout on the headquarters' roof, with a siren. There had been a bombing-attack during the afternoon. The lookout had promptly blown his warning siren. That much we know is true. The second bit was that Reggie had been racing down the corridor from his office, to get out and into one of his recently-dug slit-trenches. Somebody else, having much the same idea in mind, had unluckily flung a door wide open into the corridor in front of Reggie and…off to hospital as in the other stories. A good anecdote, but also apparently without foundation.

A third rumour was slightly more soberly based. Its source was a hospital doctor who came to the squadrons with an ambulance to fetch a wounded man. We cross-questioned him eagerly. He would not discuss any 'injuries', or causes for them – on that score the doc just clammed up. He said that Reggie had had a nervous breakdown and, overall, it had been considered best for him to be evacuated to Basrah in one of the 31 Squadron DC2s which had come to evacuate the women and children. Curiously, Smart had insisted on going by himself, except for the doctor. Throughout the trip he sat in a chair, with his back against the door of the locked crew-compartment, holding a loaded sten-gun across his knees. The doc commented: 'I wonder who he thought was going to get in?'

No detailed facts on his departure are recorded in the official Habbaniya records, save only to say that he was injured in an accident, and that he was air-evacuated to Basrah. That does not tally with the vivid recollections, written down at the time, of Lady Holman, who was with Smart for a few days, staying at Air House. She recalled: 'He lacked the respect of all his subordinates, mainly because he discussed with everybody, quite openly and freely, everything that was happening – together with his personal thoughts and plans – as if he was out on a picnic. Then, when the attack started he became quite hysterical. He went absolutely berserk. It was so serious that the senior doctor from the hospital gave Reggie a knockout injection so that he was totally unaware of what was going on and could be evacuated quietly. And, which is more, I actually saw him being put on the aircraft. There was no question whatever of his having been injured.'

Her records correspond in some respects with those of Marshal of the Royal Air Force Lord Tedder. After the war he confirmed in his memoirs exactly what the doctor had said to us at the time. He wrote that, as Air Commander in the Middle East he had replaced Air Vice-Marshal Smart who had broken down under the strain of events at Habbaniya; he had had doubts too, about his handling of the forces under his command.

On 29 May Reggie was evacuated from Basrah to India by boat. A private letter written from Basrah on 28 May says of the Smart family: 'They are off to India tomorrow as the AOC has had a motor accident and lost his front teeth – concussion and a cracked breast-bone, so he has been given two months sick-leave…so they have got what they wanted.'

Memory is a funny thing, but those are the stories. It is likely that the full truth will never be known. Maybe Reggie was injured at Habbaniya, perhaps at Basrah. One certainty; we never had contact with him after the first day.

Whatever the details are, the fact is that Reggie made the mind-boggling decision to strike with no clear directives to back him. Right up to the moment of the crunch, everyone above him had delicately side-stepped any real responsibility. All, using one form of weasel-wording or another, along with perhaps offering good or poor suggestions, had finally retreated behind a bland 'You decide what to do, old boy; you are the man on the spot!' True indeed, but of little real help to a man facing potential disaster against overwhelming forces, and who had been consistently refused reinforcements to counter them effectively. As some wag said later, those at the very top must have had extremely painful piles – after all that sitting on the fence. At last, Smart decided to attack the plateau without warning – in spite of having an obviously inadequate force for the job. This had pinned the Iraqi forces where they were. But, for how long? Neither he nor we were able to tell. Almost any man's nerve could have proved unequal to the strain.

From this point on a period is entered in which it is nearly impossible to identify what happened precisely when. This period lasted about a hundred hours. None of us in the flying team wrote much down, signed papers or kept records unless it was absolutely essential. Much of my flying log-book and the Servicing Schedules are blank. My instructions were all verbal and we flew, and flew, and flew. Some things we were told by the Butcher, and some we did off our own bat because we preferred him not to know. A diminishing band of pilots went on like automatons. They had a diminishing complement of aeroplanes and those which were still flying looked more and more as if they had the measles, with fabric patches rough-doped and slapped over the bullet holes.

After my first night's hoo-hah under the bed with howitzer shells and the dog, I decided I would take Frankie up flying with me. It couldn't be worse for him than being on the ground. For any pet to fly on operational sorties was utterly contrary to all known RAF rules and regulations – he might become frenzied and bite, or be scared and get mixed up with the controls, or goodness knows what else. So far as I was concerned, no one of any seniority seemed to be risking his neck if he didn't have to, so no one that mattered was close enough to see me and cause me any trouble.

Frankie got the hang of things with remarkable speed – fear is a potent teacher. It was only a couple or three sorties before he had the whole drill absolutely pat. If I carried a flying helmet he would trot along a few feet in front of me, looking right and left over his shoulders, trying to divine which aircraft I was going to fly. Also, I suspect, to make sure I didn't get away from him. When we got to one of the Oxfords, he knew precisely what to do. He stood by the door near the tail plane, waiting for it to be opened – and to be lifted in, because he wasn't tall enough to jump it. Once in, he scampered up front and stood squarely, looking out of the Plexiglas bomb-aimer's window in the nose. There he stayed, overseeing things and taking backward glances at me from time to time – in case I escaped, I suppose – till we were off the ground and hurtling away from the guns on the plateau. Having supervised adequately the lift-off and seen the ground falling away below him, he came back to the plywood floor beside my seat, curled himself up and appeared to go to sleep.

No amount of swooping and swirling about on my part disturbed him and somehow this placid creature beside me, exuding total confidence, was reassuring. When the engines were throttled back for the approach, he would promptly get up and nip back to his station at the bomb-aimer's window to oversee my landing. Only when we came to a halt would he leave his post and run aft, waiting for the door to be opened so that he could jump down.

Of course, when I was flying a Gladiator or a Gordon which had no floor upon which he could lie beside me, the unfortunate fellow went nearly bonkers. Poor Frankie, he never, ever, came to terms with my unforgivable treason in leaving him behind among the shell-bursts.

Each day's work began at 8 p.m., as soon as it was dark. Using screened torches, the Servicing teams tried to assess how many aircraft they could have flyable by dawn. We the squadron commanders, also showing no lights, worked out what could be done with as many aircraft in the air as possible, and counted warm bodies for first sorties on the morrow. Pilots and pupils, most of them, did not get away till some time after 10 p.m. to scrounge the remains of whatever meal they could find in the mess. Squadron commanders not less than two hours after that. Then bed. Everybody back to the hangars about 4 a.m. getting the programme into motion for the start at dawn, around 5 a.m.. Fly, fly, fly, till half an hour after sunset when it was too dark to see the plateau, which was 8 p.m., and the merry-go-round began again.

From that routine only certain highlights remain, and perhaps they will bear the telling.

Inevitably, some of the stories that follow will be my own. But, all the way through, bear in mind that around me were all the others, doing equal work, flying equally hard and taking equal risks – not only the aircrews but the ground-crews as well. I have no records as to what or how many medals, citations and awards went to the ground crews and the pupil-pilots at the finish but, whatever the total, it was not enough. It couldn't be. Except for the three medals specifically mentioned in this book, I know of no other award recommended by the Butcher for bravery in his School's efforts – and, after it was all over, he refused to reconsider his decision. The airmen fitters and riggers worked all through the day. They were being shelled and sometimes strafed when they were working on the ground. If they volunteered also to help out as aircrew, they were under fire and perhaps in even greater danger while they were working in the air. And then they worked virtually all night, having to shade and obscure every light – or they would promptly get fired at. Not forgetting the howitzer and field-gun shells being tossed at random into the camp every few minutes.

Whilst the guns and the forces on the plateau were our main objectives, we also made attacks on the Iraqi Air Force. Wellingtons came up from Basrah to meet us over Raschid airfield in Baghdad. We sent in dive-bombing Audaxes and Gordons while Sergeant Prickett, flying with me for he was the only trained bomb-aimer we had, master-minded pattern bombing by the Oxfords and, afterwards, took photographs. The photographs later showed that we had put twenty-nine Iraqi aircraft out of action – and we lost none. We learned, much later, that the British Embassy although they could not actually see the bombs burst, had otherwise enjoyed a grandstand view of the whole show.

On the way home from that or another raid, a pilot saw an Iraqi Pegasus-engined Audax flying away from Habbaniya on a course of roughly 65°, say, between east and north-east. John Hawtrey grabbed the opportunity and sent an aircraft flying along that same course. Its pilot also saw, forced-landed on the desert, a Northrop and a Savoia. Hot news! That same line pointed at an Iraqi airfield about seventy miles away called Ba'quba. We sent some Audaxes and some of the Gladiators to pay it a visit. There were twenty-one enemy aircraft parked there. The dive-bombers got ten and the fighters took three.

The Iraqis there had retaliated with some ground fire and one Audax got a bullet through its engine, which promptly stopped producing any helpful power to head home. The pilot glided as far away as he could, and then landed successfully on hard sandy desert. Although he was some miles distant, it was not long before enemy troops arrived in a truck to take the two crewmen prisoner. Having had their airfield roundly and soundly beaten up, they were pretty unfriendly and took the opportunity to vent their ill-temper on our two men. They were stripped naked and had their hands tied behind their backs. Then they were severely beaten. Next they were made to run all the way to the airfield, barefoot, being struck all the way with staves, rifle-butts and any other weapon to hand. The crew, however, counted themselves very lucky that that was all they suffered. They did not have their genitals slashed off – a very painful, messy and unpleasant way of dying and a not uncommon fate of prisoners in that country in those days – a fate which we all feared greatly.

My deputy in the Gordon flight, Horse Evans, had collected several flesh wounds on the first day, but he adamantly refused to stop flying. I did not try and dissuade him for I needed every pilot I could get. His 'stick-and-string' Gordons were doing yeoman service, removing pin-point targets on the plateau. It was he, on his own, who devised the method of attack. It was horrifying to watch, but extremely successful.

First, he fitted 250lb bombs. Those bombs have special safety devices, put there expressly to ensure that the bomb must fall at least 200 feet before becoming 'live' and exploding – so as not to blow the aircraft above to bits. Evans had fuses fitted to give a seven-second delay between impact and explosion. When he was ready for take-off, he removed the special safety devices. This totally forbidden and near-lunatic removal meant that if there were to be any fault or mishap causing a bomb to come off its rack, on the tarmac or during take-off, Horse and his stalwart pupil-gunner (together with anyone else standing nearby) would be blown up – just seven seconds later. Now, he was ready for the off.

Horse, having gone through the usual hair-raising take-off pattern, would climb steadily to about 3,000ft over the airfield. From there he could take his time picking out and confirming the precise spot where his target was. Then, dropping a wing, he would roll the machine over and pull down into a near-vertical dive – reaching the giddy speed, for a Gordon of that age, of about 200mph and with its bracing wires between the wings screaming like a banshee. Pulling out as late as he dared, and using as cover every available gully or fold in the ground, Horse would 'lay' his bomb like an egg, from a height of about six to ten feet. The Gordon, with its highly unusual speed, and seven seconds grace, got just far enough away before the 'egg' hatched, as it were. Horse admitted that, even so, the thump from behind him made his teeth rattle. The Iraqi gunners, presumably knowing what was coming after the first demonstration, steadfastly refused to stand up and fire back with machine-gun or rifle. Horse assured me that the business 'must be quite safe really you know, Sir, because Gordon damage from ground-fire is virtually negligible!'

If the Iraqis brought up machine guns, or riflemen, too close to the airfield for our comfort, the RAF armoured cars could sort them out in no time. A serious problem arose, however, when under cover of darkness the enemy brought up a pom-pom and hid it out of our sight just behind the brick-built markers' hut on the rifle-range. It would have opened up one of our old armoured cars like a can of beans if one of them had gone to try and sort it out. And it was slap under the normal approach for the airfield. The staid DC2s, unable to sweep and swoosh around smartly as we did, would have been sitting ducks.

Horse tackled the problem willingly and at once. We on the airfield could not see the gun itself because of the hut; they, of course, could not see us, and Horse made that work for him. I shall never forget seeing Horse coming down over the camp, virtually standing the Gordon on its nose above our heads, and with his bombs clearly outlined under the bottom wing and pointing straight at us. I remember praying earnestly that he did not have his hand on the bomb-release lever for, if he tweaked it, we would have been directly underneath as they fell. He flattened out incredibly low and streaked away from us across the airfield at no more than three or four feet, completely hidden from the pom-pom. He lifted his Gordon up just enough to clear the building – and laid his egg neatly on the far side. Horse swore, by all that is holy, he could see the looks of horror on the gun-crew's faces. Whether or not he scored a direct hit, no one could tell. Nevertheless, the Iraqis immediately ceased to derive further pleasure from that particular gun-location.

Forty miles or so to the south of Baghdad lies the little village of Al Musaiyib, on the Euphrates. There the enemy had a rifle factory. It was not a major target but half a dozen Audaxes paid it a short and unfriendly visit, setting it on fire.

One of my Oxfords, on its normal hairy take-off run, was damaged by a shell-burst and came to rest on the airfield. The crew, very sensibly, decided that discretion was the better part of valour. Being in full view of the enemy, they took no action to try and save it. They sprinted flat-out for the hangars. It was only a few moments before it had been hit by another shell and set on fire. It was not so much the loss of yet another Oxford which depressed me, though that was bad enough, but it looked as though the Iraqi reactions and gunnery were improving, both in speed and accuracy. That was very bad news. Further, of course, the wreck could not be cleared away. It made yet another hazard for our take-off runs. It added to the shell-holes, and Wellington and tractor carcasses – we felt we had enough problems out there already.

Capitalising on my earlier photographic survey experience in India, I was asked to make quite a lot of local photo-reconnaissance trips. Some were to identify and photograph suspected gun-positions on the other side of the camp, across the river Euphrates which ran along our northern boundary. Some were to pick out, and to confirm by interpretation, possible nearby encampments which were used as bases for high-speed, overnight, 'there-and-back' supply runs to the plateau. I also took and laid out a new photo-mosaic map of the complete plateau; this was so that the Butcher could have better and updated target identification, and for him to allocate new targets.

These photographic sorties were, mostly, a wonderful relief. The Iraqi Air Force already seemed pretty nervous about coming our way, and we also kept a Gladiator on patrol. Floating around over Habbaniya for an hour or two, at 5,000ft, above the range of gunfire, in the cooler air, away from the shelling, it felt like the most delightful and safest place in all Iraq. Conversely, photo-trips *away* from the camp, with no protective Gladiator, in a fragile plywood Oxford, yellow-painted as a training machine to make it more noticeable, were scary as hell.

Another important duty was to pick out and try to destroy, if possible, the actual vehicles which might be working from the local bases to transport supplies, encouragement, and even reinforcements to the plateau during darkness. An Oxford pilot of mine, making one of these attacks, was hit by three bullets – one through his thigh, one through his shoulder and one through his wrist. He very calmly broke off the engagement, stepped out of the pilot's seat and handed the aircraft over to the pupil-pilot who had been acting as his bomb-aimer. Next, he bandaged himself up with his first-aid kit as best he could. He took over the aircraft again to come home and do the usual dicey approach and landing, and get the machine down – intact, except for the extra holes from bullets. After landing, and although his wounds were by no means light, he courageously insisted that he was willing to carry on. The docs refused to let him fly again with that muscle-damage. Regretfully I agreed with them. Regretfully? Yes, because I was yet another pilot short. He was evacuated by the next DC2 to come from Basrah. How much longer could we last?

Habbaniya had never been designed as a strategic post in a modern hostile environment, which it had suddenly become. Water, sewage, electric power systems were all unduplicated, and loss of any one would become catastrophic within twenty-four hours. Our bombing and machine-gun strafing by day had certainly greatly reduced the shelling, but on the second night it was painfully apparent that the enemy artillery was using the freedom of darkness to step up their hammering of our camp. They threw in, roughly, a shell a minute. Something would have to be done to reduce risks from this nocturnal Iraqi barrage – and the only possible answer was to fly by night.

John Hawtrey and I put our heads together to try and dream up a way of doing it. Obviously, there was no way that we could improvise or use any kind of flarepath. Lights that the pilots could see would also be a magnificent target for the Iraqi gunners. However, the moon was in the sky for the first half of the night. John and I agreed that several of his best Audax pilots could, with a few hand-torches hidden behind the trees for guidance, fiddle their way off the polo-pitch, and back down again on to it later, by moonlight alone. An unpleasant task, though acceptable. So far so good.

But, what about after the moon had set? There were about six hours without a moon. Any machine would have to have a landing-light for the moment of touch-down – and that meant the Oxfords, for only they had landing-lights. Next, the polo-ground wasn't long enough for their landing-run. They needed more space than that. Was it conceivable that Oxfords might attempt sorties from the main airfield, in pitch darkness?

The airfield's shape and length meant that the final approach would have to be right over the plateau, packed with Iraqis. On the other hand, with no moon and some luck, they ought not to be able to pick out the machine just above them in the pitch-black. And they might be keeping their heads well down in case a bomb fell. And the landing-lights would be used only for the few seconds of touching down. John Hawtrey asked dubiously, 'Could it be done?' How could I know? It sounded like a truly lousy idea, but what else could be offered except to try and find out – using that overworked cliché of 'Suck it and see!' We told the Butcher, who made no comment.

There were only three pilots for the Oxfords who had any operational night flying experience, and I was one of them. Some others had done a bit of night flying, but not a lot. Taking turns, if a workable pattern of flying could be found, three two-hour patrols would be enough for the black-time, and the lucky last man could land by dawn-light. If they continued to shell the camp, the gun-flashes would give us pin-point targets to drop bombs on. Otherwise, we had our eight anti-personnel bombs and dropping one every fifteen minutes, we felt, would encourage the enemy to keep their heads down. We three pilots worked out details together. I would take the first sortie and, if I didn't get back in one piece, the other two could assume that the idea was even more ridiculous than first thought – and stay on the ground.

Our method is interesting to recall. I began the first black-night flight shortly before midnight and ten minutes after the setting of the moon. Outside the cockpit, all was indigo darkness. After starting up I was guided through the gates by shielded torches. Then we were on our own. I braked to a standstill. Even with my cockpit-lighting extinguished, partly to preserve my night-vision and partly because the glow might be visible from outside, there was nothing whatever for me to see – not even the packed sand we stood on. Only the luminous instruments on the fascia-board and some stars above. Next, setting the throttles for slightly fast tick-over, the brakes were released which allowed the aircraft to roll forward, along the compass course we had worked out beforehand. We knew we were rolling because Prickett, lying in the nose, could just see the sand moving under him in the starlight. Also, I could feel a slight shaking from the rough surface but I could see no movement which, on the ground and looking out of the windscreen at nothing, felt odd as hell. Prickett timed us and we let her roll for four and a half minutes exactly. We had estimated that after that time we should be near to the far side of the airfield – and close to the plateau. There was no means of checking for we could still see nothing outside. After that time, at least we had been lucky enough not to run into the ditch along the far edge.

I was very conscious of the fact that, if the Iraqis guessed from the noise what was happening and were brave enough, they could nip down from the plateau and, running towards the sound of our engines, get quite close enough unseen to toss a hand-grenade at us. Or, for that matter, to fling rocks through the cockpit windows.

Turning on to our new compass heading, I opened the throttles for a blind take-off. It was total reliance on the luminous paint of my instruments. The tension increased horribly as we gathered speed. Somewhere about half way across were carcasses of the blown-up Wellington bomber and the tractor. To hit or miss was pure luck. A hit with full tanks would turn us into a flaming wreck. A bit further on was the Oxford skeleton and beyond that at the far end was the ten foot dike, with the cushioning of a brick wall. If we had made even a minor miscalculation and turned towards it too early, that too would wrap us up in a burning ball.

As soon as I dared, I lifted her off, and took a deep breath. Once clear of the ground, we climbed rapidly. At 1,000ft the darkness was not quite so intense. Under a canopy of brilliant stars we could just distinguish trees and roads from featureless desert, water from sand. Prickett, through the nose-window, could just about tell where we were. I switched on the cockpit lights and for the next two hours we criss-crossed the plateau, dropping the occasional bomb to keep their eyes open and their heads down. Having them stay awake to become as tired as we were would be no bad thing for us anyway. Whether it was from the Audax efforts earlier in the moonlight, or our own, or both, we had seen hardly any gun-flashes so hopefully the effort had been worth while.

Half an hour before the time came for landing I turned off my cockpit-lighting to regain maximum night-vision. At 1,000ft we could just pick out, in the starlight, the serpentine twists of the river. Guided by Prickett, I followed it along the side furthest away from the plateau. He, peering out of the Plexiglas nose, was able to lead me so as to pass, facing in the right direction, over a distinctive river bend which half-encircled the camp. That was my calculated start-point. Having overflown it, I throttled back and began a steady and gentle right-handed descending turn in the inky blackness. It felt like flying with my head in a black velvet bag, with some luminous paint on its inside. I could visualise, uncomfortably, the Iraqis below, peering up into the night, hearing us – but unable to see us, I hoped. By the time the altimeter read 250ft, we were facing the opposite direction. So far, so good. If all was well, we should now be over the lip of the plateau, with the airfield ahead of us. In any case, being just above the enemy troops, there was no question of turning any lights on yet. Count another ten seconds – and don't hurry over it. Now, assume that the plateau, stacked with enemy soldiery, had passed behind us.

Had we miscalculated, or not? This was the moment of truth. So, descend another 100ft, down to just above the airfield level. If we were too early, a fatal crash was but a couple of seconds away for we should hit the plateau. If too late, it could mean running into the 10ft dike at the other end of the airfield – if we had not collided with the remains of the burned-out tractor and aircraft corpses on the way. Down we went.

When the altimeter showed 50ft without a sudden explosive halt, the plateau, for sure, was behind us. Now, what was ahead? I switched on the landing-light and saw hard sand below. Seconds later the road round the airfield passed beneath, and then the ditch. Thanks to Prickett and perhaps to my Guardian Angel also it had come out all right, so far. All that remained now was snap the throttles shut and land straight ahead. Knowing a thousand or more pairs of eyes could be watching from the plateau, seeking any chance for their owners to grab their rifles and fire, I switched off the landing light the instant the wheels touched the ground. On luminous instruments alone we braked to a standstill, grateful that we had not discovered one of the obstructions.

The piling up of stress and those final few moments which had held the prospect of a fatal crash any second – and no way of taking any avoiding action – had been totally absorbing. The intense concentration had completely shut out all other sensations. It had not been truly frightening and I had been calm while it was going on. But, now, reaction set in. I was literally shaking. My breath heaved as if I had been running. My eyes didn't focus properly and my ears were singing. Sweat was pouring down between my shoulder-blades making my back tingle with an ice-cold sensation. It sounds stupid now and you may think it cowardly in a way, for the danger was over and I was more-or-less safe – but those were the physical sensations. It must have been a couple of minutes, sitting motionless in the cockpit, before Prickett spoke on the intercom, 'What's up? Are you okay?' I shook my head to clear it. 'Fine,' I answered, 'no problems.'

Pulling my wits together and, looking towards the hangars, I could pick out the flicker of someone signalling in the distance with a hooded torch. We taxied in.

The second and subsequent black-landings were much less horrible somehow – I suppose one can get accustomed to anything.

Although I did my best to watch for signs of mental and physical exhaustion in all my crews, I did not always detect them early enough. One of the pilots, after his nerve-twisting experience of getting back on the ground at night with no lighting to guide him, got out of his Oxford with his hands trembling. Shaking his head from side to side and with his eyes shut, I heard him mutter, almost under his breath, 'Don't ask for that again…not again…that's enough.' I didn't ask him again. How could I? And I didn't think badly of him for it. Worse followed. The third black-night-pilot either taxied out too slowly, or not for long enough. He turned his machine for take-off too early, leaving himself too short a take-off run. He *nearly* made it, but by a whisker his wheels clipped the top of the ten-foot dike. His machine somersaulted into the marshes beyond, where it caught fire. That was the end of him, and his crew – and of yet another Oxford.

There was no going-back now. There was no alternative. The task was vital and had to be done. It felt like a real-life version of the roundelay where ten green bottles hang upon the wall, and in each verse one more bottle will accidentally fall. Till there are no bottles left. If anyone had been able to give me a choice, to continue or not, I should have said 'No', firmly and clearly. But there was no one else to do it.

After four hours of fitful sleep, Prickett and I were airborne for fifteen of the next forty hours. Two day sorties, two black-night sorties, two more day sorties, and another black-night sortie. But, frankly, I chickened out of the last black landing; I nursed the Oxford up there for an extra hour – three hours in all – and eased her back on to the ground in the grey half-light of dawn – touching down as far away from the plateau as I could get.

The shelling at night was significantly reduced, but at a price so far as I was concerned. Administratively, the Butcher was doing masterly work, keeping our supplies of bombs, ammunition and fuel going in spite of the amazing difficulties in transport and shell-damage. He was, however, disappointing us as a pilot. Our stock of irreplaceable pilots was dwindling inexorably. I was young, intolerant, and very fatigued from flying almost without respite throughout the twenty-four hours. I became more and more frustrated each time I saw him, sitting there in his ops-room, poring over my photo-mosaics, hour after hour from one day to the next, plotting targets seen and suggested to him, and then giving them back to us for the next man who came in.

It led me to an action I should never have taken. Curiously, and in common with many forty to forty-five year old pilots of that era, the Butcher hardly ever flew. He had certainly not done so during the month since I had arrived. Our desperate shortage of pilots led us to feel we should share and share alike. We needed every extra pair of hands we could get. Before me sat an instructor of the highest category – A.1 – and graded fully fit medically for any duty. I pressed him to take a sortie – in an aircraft bombed up and ready to go. He claimed he was too busy to spare the time for it. Finally, I said 'Sir, you have not yet seen the top of the plateau. I, and your pilots, believe you should. My aircraft is outside, engines running, and ready for the targets you gave me a few moments ago. Come with me and you will be back here in twenty minutes, or less.' Again he demurred and I urged him, leaning upon the morale factors of help and encouragement to our hard-pressed crews – and hinting at desirability of a personal example. He turned to me, in obvious distress as I looked at him. My expression was hard. At last he gave in. 'All right,' he said, he would come with me on a trip, as my passenger.

Above the plateau, we had done a couple of bombing runs when suddenly he listened and asked: 'What's that pht-pht-phtting noise?' I replied 'Machine-gun or rifle bullets, going past outside, close by.' He looked out of the window at the wing and, at that very instant, a line of bullet holes was punched up through its surface. 'My God!' he shouted, 'We've been hit! Go back and land at once.' As captain of the aircraft I refused this demand and we completed the remaining runs of our sortie. He sat beside me with his hands on his knees and staring straight ahead. He organised his Ops Room well, but it was the only occasion that he ever left the ground during the whole campaign, even though his medal ribbons clearly showed that twenty years before he had certainly done his full share. At that time, a tired and obstinate young officer felt his older boss deserved what he had received. Now, I deeply regret what I did to him.

On the third day, unexpectedly, four Blenheim twin-engined fighters of 203 Squadron arrived from Egypt. Nobody had given them any suitable briefing, or warning of what to expect. One must assume that with Reggie Smart gone, no one else properly in charge and all Embassy communications cut off, there was no one in Egypt who really understood what was going on in our neck of the woods. Be that as it may, they were completely unaware of our inhospitable neighbours on the plateau, and came in to land doing normal approaches. Three of the Audaxes, which happened at the time to be flying up there, saw their normal approaches with deep alarm. They did their best to keep enemy heads down by dive-bombing ahead of the Blenheims. One of those pilots swore blind he had come in through the dust of a 250lb bomb. True or false, three of the four were found after they landed to have bullet holes in them. Luckily the damage was minor and could be repaired quickly.

The Blenheim pilots had been staggered to see officers and airmen rushing out on to the airfield waving their arms and making frantic signals which could only mean 'Come in and get behind the hangars, QUICKLY!' Very soon, after a few shells had landed, their opinions matched ours exactly.

We repaired the bullet holes and next morning we had a Blenheim, with its four machine guns, on standing patrol. The Iraqis obligingly sent in two of their Pegasus-engined Audaxes to strafe and bomb us in the camp. Plainly, they must have seen the wicked shape of the Blenheim fighter for they both turned tail and fled. One went flat out for ground level, hotly pursued by a fast overtaking Blenheim. The killing burst came just above the river and the Audax dived straight in. Muddy water was flung up all over the Blenheim's windscreen. Everybody in the camp who wasn't flying had a grandstand view. When the Blenheim returned to patrol and sedately waggled his wings, even the enemy on the plateau must have heard the cheer that we sent up.

We suspected that the other Audax, which escaped, must have seen the performance and told his chums about it after he got home. Certainly, the frequency and strength of the enemy daylight raids fell off dramatically. And, as they didn't night-fly, this was very welcome.

What more could we do? Outside the Officers Mess were two field-guns of First World War vintage. They were duly stripped and cleaned; legend has it that twenty-two coats of paint were removed – one for each year they had been standing there as ornaments. The only ammunition for such archaic pieces was in India, but 31 Squadron once more came to our rescue. They flew in shells with their DC2s. Rumour was strong that the gun-team would be a wholly RAF one, composed solely of elderly Wing Commanders, some Warrant Officers and Flight Sergeants – all of them ex-Army with Gunner experience; finally, their leader would be the Butcher, who too had been a Gunner Officer of the same era. We were quite disappointed when our local ground-forces took them over.

We later learned that they had had a tremendous effect on our enemies which far outweighed their material achievements. The soldiers, up on the plateau, were convinced that guns in quantity were now being flown in from Basrah. Firing at us without riposte was all very well, but to have us firing back, over open sights – particularly when added to our bombing and strafing – proved to be a dreadful blow to their morale.

What with shelling, bombing, strafing and ground-fire, consumption of aircraft was high. During the evening of the fourth day, from my twenty-seven Oxfords at the outset, only four could be rated as 'flyable' – and one of those sported well over seventy fabric patches pasted over bullet holes from thirty-five bullets – on the way in and on the way out. The Audax, Gladiator and Gordon squadrons were no better off. In addition to the dead pilots and those in hospital or evacuated to Basrah, four others from my original nineteen had had to be taken off flying because their nerves had cracked. We were getting very near the knuckle, even though the airmen were working miracles to get our flying colanders back in shape for the morning. They reckoned that next day I might have eight or nine which could get off the ground.

On the fifth morning – 6 May – the daily reconnaissance Audax came back hot-foot from the road across the marshes with the alarming warning that considerable enemy reinforcements of guns, men and armoured cars were approaching the plateau from the direction of Baghdad. This alone was daunting news but also we received our heaviest raid to date from the Iraqi Air Force at about 10 a.m. It seemed that they had determined to finish us off, once and for all. This was IT! Could we halt them? The reinforcements had to be broken up short of the plateau, or we should be finished off within hours. We girded up our loins for a maximum-effort strike without pause, like the first day; to hit and hit and hit again – in hope.

Then, curiously, the Iraqis on the plateau decided at the same time that they were going to leave. Why? We cannot tell. Maybe they were unaware of the reinforcements coming in; perhaps the soldiers reckoned that their pay, then worth about one English pound for every couple of months, was inadequate compensation for what we had been dishing out to them. Anyway, whatever it was, they fled, streaming off the higher ground, down the escarpment and on to the road for Baghdad. Their departure was no orderly withdrawal. It was nothing less than a rout.

As the first vehicles from the plateau going away met those of the reinforcements from Baghdad coming in, they closed up and stopped nose to tail instead of stopping in dispersed formation. This was just when every flyable Audax, Gordon, Gladiator and Oxford fell upon them. We threw in every machine that could be prevailed upon to take off. We *had* to win, without fail. And 'to win' was to prevent them somehow, by hook or by crook, by fair means or foul, from regrouping and returning to the plateau, with the reinforcements or without.

Having been regretfully and nervously husbanding our ever-diminishing resources for the previous thirty-six hours or so, we went back to flat-out effort – bomb and fire in minimum time, race home, don't stop engines, reload, race back, and so on – and to hell with the cost. Down below us it was mayhem.

Assuredly, the Iraqis had meant serious business. At about 5 p.m. we received our second heavy Iraqi bombing raid of the day. Those two raids together cost us on the ground two Oxfords, one Gladiator, one Audax, seven people killed and eight more wounded.

At the moment of the second raid it was my turn to make a formal report to Butcher in his ops-room, while Prickett took his turn to put on a fresh bomb-load. As I talked, I heard the roar of a diving aircraft and the ear-splitting crashes as a stick of bombs fell, not too far away. When I got back to my Oxford, Arthur Prickett was lying on the ground underneath it, on his side with his knees bent up to his stomach. Five out of eight bombs had been loaded; three were still lying on the ground. I remember noting the engines were still running. I crawled below the fuselage and rolled him on to his back. His eyes were open and his face had that particular yellow-blue tint which appears in seconds when the blood stops flowing. By that stage of the war it told me precisely what I was looking at. One more friend and colleague had gone from my life.

To check, I took his wrist, and also felt for his heartbeat. There was no pulse. There was a small wound just over his heart and not much blood. I looked at him, thinking that if it had been my turn to reload, instead of his, I should have been lying there. Looking up, I muttered a little prayer for him, completely lost in the noise of running engines. 'Please, dear God, take his soul in care and kindness.' Then, looking aside, I shouted loud, uncouth curses at the bestiality of war. It made me feel a tiny bit better. I pulled his body to one side and sent someone with instructions to tell the Butcher, and call an ambulance to take Arthur Prickett's remains away.

A check of the aircraft showed there was no significant new damage. I loaded the remaining three bombs and told the nearest pupil-observer that he was my bomb-aimer from now on. He had the splendid British name of Smith. We took off for the next raid. The attack on the road-convoys lasted about two hours. We made 139 aircraft sorties and, when the last aircraft left, its pilot reported that the road was a strip of flames, several hundred yards long. There were ammunition limbers exploding, with cars and lorries burning by the dozen. We lost one Audax shot down.

For the first time, our own ground forces from our camp were able to make a sortie outside the camp and they also played a satisfying part. They took 408 prisoners including 27 officers; the total Iraqi casualties on that day alone, including prisoners, were later assessed as 1,000. We lost 1 officer and 6 British soldiers killed, with 2 officers and 10 British soldiers wounded.

That night was strangely and blissfully quiet. No shelling. No flying. Frankie was a bit miffed at no longer being allowed into my bed. Next morning, the reconnaissance Audax reported that there was no sign of life whatever on the plateau. Strangely, even after their resounding successes of the day before, our ground forces firmly declined to go up there and 'capture' it. They said it might be a trick, a booby-trap. We put on a short air-attack to see if we could start a rabbit, but no results. Finally, it was the RAF armoured cars which went up there and confirmed the place was empty. By lunchtime, it had been formally recaptured; we never learned if it was the RAF or our Army who laid claim to having done the job. Later, a few enemy machine-gunners were located in the little village of Dhibban, down by the river just east of the camp, but our ground forces had them cleaned up before the evening.

During those 5 hectic days our hastily armed, outdated training machines had dropped well over 3,000 bombs, totalling over 50 tons, and we had fired 116,000 rounds of ammunition. The ops-room had recorded 647 sorties, but we had completed, unrecorded, many more than that. Both John and I had sent off occasional sorties for some good purpose without telling the Butcher and a lot of the Audax pilots never bothered to spend time and energy walking from the polo-pitch to the Ops Room, just to tell the Butcher what they had done. They just got on with the job, which was to harass the enemy wherever and whenever he was found.

Our losses were 13 killed and 21 too badly wounded to carry on – and 4 more grounded from nerves gone. That was from the School alone. Most of those who joined us from other formations in the camp, to come and work in the hot-seats, are not included because they were never recorded by the Butcher; they did not appear on his 'official' rolls.

But, and a great *but*, the plateau was now clear. We could sleep in quiet. Aircraft could be repaired in the patchy shade, *inside* the riddled hangars. Moreover, our private army now had, in working order, six howitzers with 2,400 shells, an 18-pounder gun, a tank, 10 modern armoured cars, 3 pom-poms with 2,500 shells, 34 Bren guns, 11 Vickers guns, 340 rifles and 500,000 rounds of ammunition. We felt that if any Iraqi durst show a whisker over the edge of the plateau he would get a very close shave.

Our greatest benefit however, was free use of the airfield. We could clear away the wreckage of the two burnt-out aircraft, and the tractor. Best of all, it meant that we could use pupils, competent pilots in the later stages of their training, as captains of aircraft. Admittedly, many had done no advanced training; that is, they had never dropped even a practice-bomb or fired a front-gun round. Others were barely beyond the solo stage. But, all were mad keen to take a part bigger than just 'crew member'. Now they had their chance to take on a bit of our flying-load.

We had to impose some restrictions on them of course, to prevent them committing suicide by exceeding their personal skills. For example, the pupils flying Audaxes could only do dive-bombing and armed reconnaissance. Using a front-gun is a different kettle of fish. Knowing how to fire late and close enough for accuracy – and yet to pull-out early and high enough to avoid hitting the ground – is a very tricky piece of judgement indeed! Therefore we forbade them air-to-ground front-gunning. It would have been far too dangerous in their inexperience. We didn't have the time or chance to teach them and we couldn't afford to lose them. The pre-war RAF's macabre sense of humour was illustrated by a human skull on the chimney-piece of the Officers' Mess at Basrah; on its polished plinth was a little brass plate engraved with the words 'Winner of the 1937 Front-Gunnery Contest'.

The Oxford pupils could make almost any kind of level-flying bombing-raid. Some they could do on their own, working it out as they went along. Most, however would do pattern-bombing with a leader. The 'leader' for this purpose was to be the young man I took on to fly with me in place of Sergeant Prickett. On the books he was still Aircraftman Smith, Observer-Under-Training.

At the end of the campaign he had become so proficient as a bomb-aimer that the rest of his training was waived; he was promoted Sergeant and posted straight to an operational squadron. The squadron found Smith a bit startling. Sergeant Smith came to them straight from school as an embryo bomb-aimer. Embryo be damned! Inspection of his flying log-book before doing a first flight with them showed he already had about twenty live operational bombing-sorties under his belt – almost a full 'tour on ops' – before he had even been awarded his wings!

That first quiet evening, I spent in the mess celebrating with John Hawtrey, swilling down whiskies like there was no tomorrow. Together we sang lustily that fine old marching song: '*John Brown's body lies a-mouldering in the grave*'. It was partly because we both thought we knew the tune and partly in homage to those of our well-liked colleagues whom we knew only too well were already 'a-mouldering' – and the whisky had a lot to do with it too. Our singing, I fear, became steadily louder and flatter.

Suddenly, John stopped. He said, earnestly, slurring his words a little and carefully tapping my chest with one finger, 'Do you realise, my good friend, what has just struck me? No? Then I'll tell you. During our horrible last five days, not one senior officer from Air Headquarters, nor one of the padres sheltered in the hospital, ever came on to my polo-pitch, or down to your airfield, to give us an encouraging word or to comfort the wounded.'

I nodded sagely. John was truly indignant about it, but frankly I couldn't have cared less. I imagined that now the enemy had run away, it was all over bar the shouting. What else mattered?

John ordered two more whiskies, to lubricate our vocal cords for the next two verses of *John Brown's body*.

Eleven
Germany Moves

After the discussion between Hitler and von Ribbentrop at the beginning of May, Colonel Junck was told to pull out of France and to report to the *Kriegs Ministerium* or, in English terms, the War Office. Having packed up his job he duly arrived in Berlin, doubtless wondering what lay in store for him. He learned he was to attend a conference with two big wheels in the Luftwaffe. One was General Jeschonnek, Chief of Air Force General Staff and the other was General von Waldau, Chief of Air Force Directing Staff. Junck must have wondered what he, a mere Colonel, was going to do for these Luftwaffe 'big guns'.

General Jeschonnek gave him his briefing. Junck learned with surprise and satisfaction that he was going to command the German forces of the Luftwaffe in Iraq. A special Commando was going to be formed for him, which would also have his own name as part of its title, 'SonderkommandoJunck'.

He was informed that, even at that moment, an approach was being made on his behalf to the Turks for an agreement to the transit of *matériel* through Turkey. Regrettably however, the Turks appeared to be dragging their feet because (or so he was told) they were scared of the Russians and the British reacting. Naturally, with the Balkan campaign already in full swing and Hitler setting enormous store by the success of *Barbarossa* (which was still under wraps) an early Russian reaction was to be avoided if humanly possible. Nevertheless, they said, the Turkish hesitation was not really a crucial matter because the French Vice-Premier, in the person of Admiral Darlan in Paris, was lending his support. He had already agreed that they would provide weapons for the Iraqis, and that they would make staging facilities available for both Germans and Italians via Damascus in Syria.

The necessary aircraft would be found for him which, they proposed, could stage through Athens, Rhodes, and Damascus. His force was going to be a 'limited number' – a *schwarm* of Me110 fighters and He111 bombers. He would also have a light-aircraft for communications purposes and some Junkers 52 transport machines. Hitler himself had already given his personal instructions that every man was to be a volunteer. Also that the aircraft were to carry Iraqi markings, or none at all. Their base would be at Mosul, about 240 miles north of Baghdad.

Poor Junck! At no time did anybody mention von Ribbentrop's proposal, that two whole squadrons of bombers and fighters should go. Presumably it was due to Hitler's overriding fiat, the pressures in the Balkans – and the shadows of *Barbarossa*.

There were many other problems, but General Jeschonnek emphasised: 'The Führer desires a Heroic Gesture.' Not unreasonably, Junck asked, politely, what on earth was meant in military terms by a 'Heroic Gesture'? The reply he got was:

> *An operation which would have a significant effect, leading eventually perhaps to an Arab rising, in order to start a Jehad, or Holy War against the British.*

Finally, he was told that Raschid Ali, Chief of the Iraqi National Defence Government, had especially asked for the return of Dr Grobba who had been working for the Germans in Baghdad over many years. Dr Grobba would be returning as soon as possible; he was to be in place by mid-May. He would be able to act in a liaison capacity with Raschid Ali, so as to have maximum impact with the Iraqi forces.

It must have seemed wildly exciting to Junck. He, a Colonel, would have his personal force, carrying his name, in a foreign country; his own *schwarm* of aircraft, responsible to him for their operations, working in conjunction with the Head of State himself, Raschid Ali, in Iraq – and the prospect maybe of triggering off a major Arab uprising against their common enemy – the British.

He could not know, yet, that there was a sinister omen for his mission. He had reported to Berlin, for briefing upon his Heroic Gesture, on 6 May. This was the very day that the air-attacks by the Flying Training School had achieved complete rout of the Iraqi Army on the plateau. They had fled in disarray, carrying with them a mortal dread of British aircraft. A fear which, magnified in the telling, would soon spread throughout the whole Iraqi Army. So great was their fear that Junck was destined to get no effective fighting support whatsoever from the Iraqi forces.

Twelve
Clearing Up: Days 7-15

The Butcher was delighted to get a signal from the Prime Minster:

> *Your vigorous and splendid action has largely restored the situation. We are watching the grand fight you are making. All possible aid will be sent.*

We had been feeling very cut off. Doubtless our 400 KORRs, our RAF armoured cars and the 1,000 Assyrian levies would have acquitted themselves magnificently if the Iraqi Army had steeled itself sufficiently to do its job properly. Nevertheless, our forces for resisting a determined attack were pathetically small. Delighted with Churchill's signal, we of course imagined that a fine and cohesive fighting army unit from Egypt had been launched forth with all speed as soon as it became known that we were under duress – and long before we began to be shelled. Succour, with tanks and guns, had to be almost on our doorstep.

Ignorance is bliss. It would have been a grave blow to our morale had we known that, far from being on our doorstep, nothing would leave the shores of the Mediterranean before 11 May – five days after we had defeated the hostile army by ourselves.

It was only after battle had been joined that Whitehall decided, on 2 May, that Iraq Command should revert from India to the Middle East. The Army Commander in Chief in the Middle East, General Wavell, was somewhat sour about it, and demurred. Had Iraq not been safely handed over to India Command a couple of months earlier? And had he not already got Greece and almost certainly Crete too on his hands? He was still pressing for reliance upon diplomatic pressure. In any case, he urged, even if he were to send a force immediately to relieve Habbaniya, as Churchill had required because the Basrah forces were cut off by floods from dikes breached by the Iraqis, it would be too little and too late.

Wavell was no fool. I cannot believe he was aware of the Germans' promise of financial and military backing for Iraq, and Raschid Ali's firm undertaking of 18 *April* to make Habbaniya available to the Axis forces, having already taken it from us. And their joint desire to boot us out of Iraq. It must have been misjudgement based on inadequate Intelligence information. Nevertheless, history records that Wavell's reluctance to react militarily in Iraq, right or wrong, was one of the reasons why he fell into disfavour with Churchill and was ultimately promoted away and replaced as the Middle East Army Commander by General Auchinlek, who had made at least some effort to help.

On 6 May, Whitehall assured him that 'there was an excellent chance of restoring the situation by bold action if it is not delayed.' It fascinates me that Whitehall had obtained that information from the decrypt of a cypher which the Italian Legation sent from Baghdad to Rome. Moreover, they had it before it came from any British source. However, if we remember that the British Embassy was silenced, there was no proper command or commander at Habbaniya – and most of the fit RAF staff officers were flying themselves into exhaustion or hospital – the scarcity of information from British sources is hardly surprising. That same cypher carried the information that Raschid Ali had failed at Habbaniya, his stocks of bombs and ammunition were exhausted and he was desperately entreating the Germans and Italians to send him bomber and fighter aircraft. It was not until three days later that the same source revealed Germany was starting to take some positive action.

Wavell dutifully began to collect troops to relieve our remote and vulnerable unit in far-off Iraq. He started the job three days after we began to be shelled. To be fair to him, he had the devil of a task in trying to put together any kind of force at all to aid us. And the diverse bunch he managed to collect was an astonishing mixture. His Majesty's Life Guards, eight RAF armoured cars snatched out of the Western Desert campaign (and under the command of that remarkable gravel-voiced Squadron Leader Cassano), Major Glubb Pasha and his Legion of Bedouin Arabs, the Royal Horse Guards, the Essex Yeomanry, RASC, 166 Field Ambulance – and many more units and parts of units to make up the team. All to be commanded by Brigadier John 'Joe' Kingstone, DSO, MC, who would then start his fighting column, 'Kingcol', on its trek from the shores of the Mediterranean to Habbaniya.

A motley team indeed it might be, but it had a tough brief. There were 450 miles to be covered, much of it over barren desert and soft sand. There were no supplies on the way and maybe no water. At the other end it might have to fight a fierce battle, with no replenishments beforehand. A daunting prospect, yet Wavell got them under way in six days – no mean feat.

Meanwhile, the School had turned its attention to the Iraqi Air Force, attacking enemy airfields and landing grounds. At first our striking force of Audaxes, Gordons and Oxfords went out in penny-packets because so few machines were fit to get airborne at all with any kind of safety. Soon, the miracle-men in Station Workshops and our own mechanics got more and more of them into flyable working order. Regularly our strikes became bigger, and better. Always we had a Gladiator or two to be our fighter-escort while we paid our visits around the Iraqi airfields. We had practically no enemy reaction against us, and so the protecting escorts could spend their unused ammunition ground-strafing. In the first two days alone we had destroyed thirteen aircraft, and damaged twenty more. These losses virtually eliminated the attacking power of the Iraqi Air Force. Very satisfying to us it was. Our enemy had fled the plateau on 6 May and over the next day or two their air force appeared to be virtually ineffective. We hoped it was because we had reduced them to impotence. Their raids were reduced to a mere two or three aircraft a day, and there was no shelling. After the previous week of near-hell, life was wonderful. Habbaniya camp itself was literally enjoying a few days of comparative peace. One could sit or lie on the lawn by the mess, lazily, with a drink. Or sit, calmly, at a table to eat one's meal.

On the 8th, an Oxford on reconnaissance was flown by one of my few remaining qualified pilots, Flight Sergeant Harry Brattan, at 3,000ft, over Ramadi village a few miles to the west of Habbaniya. We knew there were some Iraqis there, because they had packed a number of trucks into a courtyard. So I had sent Brattan off, just for a check, to see if anything showed signs of change, or if he could see something that looked like preparations for a sortie against us. Briefly, had anything changed, and if so, how?

Because everything was suddenly quiet at this juncture in the campaign and the Iraqis were lying very low; there was no point in taking risks and accordingly I was trying to reduce them to the absolute minimum. I very carefully briefed Brattan to fly at 3,000ft. He could see well enough from that height to complete the task and I knew from my previous experience on the North West Frontier of India that it would be perfectly safe from rifle or machine-gun fire. A small-calibre bullet, having climbed so high would have spent all its energy. It would by then be going too slowly to do any serious damage. But, Harry Brattan disobeyed my instructions. He had his fun, swooping around at 1,500ft and below, and learned the hard way. One solitary bullet came through the plywood cockpit-skin on the left hand side of the aircraft, struck him in the soft flesh between his hip-bone and his rib-cage and went straight on up through one of his main arteries. He bled to death in minutes.

In the back was an airman, on loan to me from his normal duty which was to work the wind-driven winches in the target-towing Gordons. To give him his full title he was 529934 Aircraftman Grade 1 Kenneth Edward William Clifton. I was using him as a rear-gunner.

He left his gun, came forward and helped to put the dead Brattan on the floor. Then, as he freely admitted later, he embarked on a youthful ambition that many non-pilots nurtured all through the war – to bring the aircraft back safely, after the pilot had been incapacitated. Clifton had only held the controls of an aircraft on one previous occasion. His efforts, seen from the ground, were hair-raising beyond belief; terrifying swoops, swirls and darts. An imminent fatal accident, must occur it seemed time after time. But he finally *did* manage to get the Oxford back and down on to the ground, all in one piece.

Having landed, he tried to taxi the aircraft back to the hangars. Taxying a twin-engined aeroplane – until you know how – is far more difficult than flying it. He was swinging crazily from side to side and it was evident, even from the hangars, that something awful had happened and the undercarriage would break within moments. So much so that a watching instructor, Kenneth Osborne-Young ran hell-for-leather out on to the airfield, waving his arms like crazy and shouting, to try and stop the pilot, whoever he was, before the undercarriage collapsed. Young said that taxying the Oxford back to the hangars was a sickening job. He, in his khaki-drill shorts, had to sit in the dead man's bucket-seat, half-full of horrible-smelling human blood and the whole cockpit seemingly awash with it.

In fact the third aircrew member in the aircraft was in reality a pupil-pilot, temporarily misemployed by me as a bomb-aimer-observer. He, well into his training, was fully competent to have flown the aircraft back easily, landed safely and taxied it in with no significant problems or risks. His personal snag at the time was that pupil-pilots had the lowest possible rank until they had been formally qualified – they were Aircraftman Grade 2.

Clifton, Aircraftman Grade 1, was the teeniest step possible above him on the RAF rank-ladder. He had used this negligible rank-advantage bluntly to order his junior, the pupil-pilot, to step aside and leave him clear to try and achieve his Walter Mitty day dream.

On one hand, half the school reckoned that Clifton had been brave – although foolhardy and astoundingly lucky – to get the aircraft down without breaking it, or worse. His fine feat deserved to be marked by an award for gallantry.

Conversely, the other half believed that Clifton's totally unnecessary risking of an all-too scarce Oxford, just to satisfy his schoolboy-type ambition, was inexcusable. He should be sentenced and punished for deliberately hazarding one of His Majesty's aircraft – not to mention its uninjured pilot-acting-bomb-aimer! He merited trial by Court Martial.

The first batch, favouring Clifton, was led by boss-man, Group Captain Butcher. The second lot, wishing to pour fire and brimstone upon poor Clifton's head was led by a very tired, unreasonable, testy and short-fused squadron leader, CO of the scarce and precious Oxfords – me.

In hindsight it is a relief to say that the Butcher cast me aside and wouldn't listen to my plaint. The airman was promoted to Leading Aircraftman Clifton and received the immediate award of the Distinguished Flying Medal – or 'DFM' for short. Although he could correctly and proudly wear the medal-ribbon above the left breast-pocket of his tunic, it did not make him qualified Aircrew, allowing him to wear aircrew 'Wings' just above it.

From then on, almost whenever he went out (wartime; in uniform of course) he was stopped and accosted fiercely by an endless succession of officers, senior NCOs and the Service Police. He, they alleged, was daring to wear the red-and-white diagonally striped ribbon of a gallantry-medal. It was the ribbon of the DFM, which is awarded exclusively to aircrew. He had no 'Wings', and therefore he could not be entitled to the medal. So, he was committing an RAF crime. Then followed a long and tedious explanation to the highly suspicious and disbelieving questioner. Clifton's story was, after all, pretty unlikely. Sometimes, he was heard to say he wished he had never been given the damned medal!

We were, perhaps unreasonably, short-tempered after Brattan's seemingly needless death. Next day we flew every Oxford – now back up to fifteen – on a demonstration over Ramadi, where Brattan had been shot. I broke off, dived down to rooftop height and dropped some leaflets suggesting they might care to surrender before we made a major air and land attack on them. There was no reaction. In truth, my threats were fairly empty. Any land-attack was quite out of the question, because of the extensive Iraqi flooding. Still, I was sufficiently tired and ill-tempered to demand revenge for my pilot, Sergeant Brattan.

That night, while Oxfords watched the Ramadi ferry in the moonlight to prevent escape, the army brought up guns. Most of them had to be on the far side of the river. Only a few could be placed on the near side, sited as close as they could get. When day broke, the School attack set fire to all their lorries in the courtyard – about thirty – and the smoke drifted fifteen miles. By mid-afternoon we and the army decided that it really wasn't worth the potential casualties, to try and capture the place. Anyway, it was in the opposite direction to our next objective, Baghdad. Further, we were dead certain that those particular Iraqis were no longer equipped, nor would they be in the mood, for any offensive action against us.

Soon after, the first of some enormously welcome aircraft-reinforcements began to arrive from Egypt. These were some more Gladiator fighters of 94 Squadron. Squadron Leader (later promoted Wing Commander) Wrightman had been placidly converting his squadron from superannuated Gladiators to Hurricanes at Ismailia on the bank of the Suez Canal. Abruptly he was told to drop everything and to take every Gladiator he could get his fingers on to Habbaniya, with pilots. He found five. The pilots he chose, besides himself, were two officers, MacRobert and Herrtage with two sergeant pilots, Smith and Dunwoodie. Records disagree as to the precise date they arrived, but it was about 11 May. The Embassy staff, with their clandestine radio, could listen only to the British broadcasts or the Iraqi and German propaganda output. As mentioned earlier, the BBC reported that we had two anti-aircraft guns – presumably a garbled interpretation of the two ornamental field-guns being stripped of paint. They also broadcast, on 10 May, that the army from Palestine had relieved Habbaniya. Actually, on that date, Wavell's column had not even set out from Nathanya, its collection point 500 miles distant on the shores of the Mediterranean. Even the hopeful Embassy suspected the veracity of that one; for one thing, why were the Iraqis still providing them with food through the good offices of Vyvian Holt, their Oriental Secretary and Councillor? Offset against the BBC information snippets were the German broadcasts, primarily for Iraqi consumption. They made lavish and factual-sounding promises hourly of Axis assistance and the miracles to be worked by Dr Grobba on his return. Soon after, the propaganda turned to what they alleged was actually being achieved now that Grobba was back in place. It boasted how very soon the British oppressors would be sent packing, indeed, departure of the British from Habbaniya had already started because that base was at the mercy of the encircling Iraqi Army and its days were numbered, and so on.

All that was in itself was depressing enough for those besieged in the Embassy, as they had no means of sifting fact from fiction, but matters had been made even worse, we learned later, by Group Captain Patrick Domville, OBE, who was on the Ambassador's staff for Intelligence duties. He had been a colonel in the 8th Hussars and on the British Military Mission to the Iraq Army before he switched the colour of his uniform.

On the night of 29 April, as soon as the Embassy realised that the Iraq Army was moving out of Washash Barracks, Domville had sent a personal telegram to the ground forces in Habbaniya. This was in addition to the signal sent by the Ambassador. He urged them to make an immediate sortie to Fallujah bridge, to block the Iraqi Army's route. As has been said, nothing actually occurred inside Habbaniya except that the General Alarm was blown. Domville, an apparently knowledgeable ex-Army officer, loudly bewailed the fact that our British ground forces had not promptly darted out of the camp and held the bridge against all comers. The Iraqi Army, he said, would then never have been allowed eighteen clear and placid hours to install themselves quietly on top of the plateau. Habbaniya's ineptitude, he claimed, had made it impossible for help from outside to be provided, and had also made it possible for the Iraqis to beleaguer the Embassy in Baghdad.

All that now goes to show now how ignorant of the true background picture, and ill-served by their Intelligence staffs, were those at the top. How would 400 stalwart King's

Own Royal Riflemen, with machine-guns and some mortars, have fared against several thousands of Iraqis – with tanks, armoured cars and field-guns? Demonstration flights, warning shots and sabre rattling were no longer of any use to us against the modernised Iraq of that time. Domville's effort to outflank Smart's authority was majestic in conception but pitiful in reality. A few hundred infantrymen could not possibly hold up a modern, well-equipped Army for even an hour or two – let alone eighteen hours! And from where would help have come – in eighteen hours? From Basrah, 300 miles away and cut off by floods? Or from Palestine, 400 miles away across the desert? Or by extensive air transport which we did not have? We, in Habbaniya, had no details as to how the Embassy was coping. For all we knew, they could have been imprisoned. Or slaughtered. We only knew that, if they were there at all, they were completely cut off. So we decided we would try and help.

An Audax was intended primarily to be an aircraft for co-operating with the army and, in the days when it was produced, radio-telephones were not carried by ground-troops in the field. So a simple method of two-way contact was used. The pilot would write what he wished to say on a piece of paper, put it in a special canvas message-bag with coloured streamers to mark it – and throw it down to the soldiers. The soldiers, in their turn would write their answer and put it in the message-bag. This would then be attached to a cord strung between two poles – or even between two rifles stuck upright with their bayonets dug into the ground. After this had been done the pilot would let down a hook, on a pole, which he could dangle a few feet below the aircraft. Then, he swooped down and caught the cord with his hook. A tricky job to do, but not too hard for a good pilot flying over flattish ground. Having hauled in the cord, with its bag, two-way contact had been established. It was a slow business, but it was simple and it worked.

Flight Lieutenant 'Stooge' Garner was a brave and skilful pilot, who knew his stuff. Several aircraft that he had flown recently had taken a lot of damage, but personally he had come through the battle practically unscathed. So we set him up to do the Embassy job. We wrote out a full set of instructions to be dropped into the Embassy compound. How to prepare two poles – broomsticks would do – and how to erect them with the cord strung between and the message-bag attached. This was all to be done on top of the Embassy building's flat roof, which was a few feet above the tops of trees in the garden. The message explained that the same pilot would plan to arrive at precisely the same time next day. We added how he, flying at 100mph, would seem to be flying straight at the top floor. In fact, he would be trying to miss it by just four to eight feet. A few feet higher, and his hook would miss the cord. A little lower, and he would crash into the roof and kill himself. Stooge knew full well that the task promised to be extremely dangerous, demanding every bit of his skills, particularly if there was a breeze causing up-draughts and down-draughts around the Embassy building. Therefore, on his behalf, we urged and implored in our message, please no spectators up on the roof to get a good view of what went on – and thereby make Stooge's task even trickier.

Stooge had no problems on the way out during the evening of 8 May. He slipped over the city at roof-top level in his Audax. All was perfectly quiet. He dropped his message-bag into the Embassy garden at 7.30 p.m. and saw somebody, who did not look like an Iraqi, run to pick it up. He came home, pleased with himself.

Next evening, a few minutes before 7.30, he went back, not too low down, and had a good look round. As instructed, the agreed signals made from bits of white sheets or towels were on the roof. All was in order. He came down low, slowly. Then he went up again, quickly. The Iraqis had obviously noted his pass-by the day before, guessed what was happening, and disapproved. It was quite quiet over the city but there was a mass of machine guns squirting at him from all round the building. Stooge was brave, but not a congenital idiot. He decided it was prudent to forget the task altogether. He hoped, not unreasonably, that no one in the Embassy would think him a coward and that the Ambassador would think it over, realise why, and agree. In fact those in the Embassy had seen perfectly clearly what had happened and were vastly relieved at Stooge's show of common sense.

Every day, at varying times, one or two Iraqi aircraft would come over low and fast to drop bombs. Also, a bit later each day, the resulting damage was checked for them by a Savoia carrying out photographic reconnaissance. He came over using oxygen, very high indeed, varied his timing, never hung around, and so he was never intercepted. One morning two Sergeants had got up to the mess for lunch and were just about to start when they heard the faint drone of an aircraft flying very high. One looked at the other and asked, 'D'you think that's a bomber?' After cocking his head and listening intently the other replied 'Oh no...that's only the old Savoia photographing.' Soon, the engine-noise became drowned by an ever-growing and uncomfortably high-pitched whistle. Instantly, both men sprang from their chairs and dived under the table for whatever security they could hope to find there. The mess got a direct hit. Its doors swung open. Windows were shattered. Bricks, plaster and glass flew everywhere. Luckily, neither of them suffered worse than a few scratches.

Slowly and deliberately, the first man crawled out from under the table and stood up. For some moments, not a word was spoken while he carefully dusted himself off and wiped the muck off his face with a handkerchief. At last, fixing his friend with an accusing eye, he said, 'Photographing? All I can say is the stupid sod has dropped his bloody camera.'

On 14 May the FTS was still basking in its hard-won peace. The Iraqi Army had never re-appeared. Their air force was limiting itself to a few sporadic tip-and-run raids. Life seemed good on that day. Somewhere out to the west our army was coming in to restore the situation and put an end to this Iraqi rebellion – for, optimistically, we still believed it was no worse than that.

One of our Blenheim-fighters landed from a routine general reconnaissance in the area of Mosul, and sprang upon us a startling and near incredible tale. The Blenheim pilot said he had been attacked by a *Messerschmitt 110* in that area! Disbelief was rife. He stuck to his story. Yes; he *did* know what a German Me110 fighter was. Yes; he *knew* they had not the range to get anywhere near there. Yes; he *knew* it was impossible – but, *there* it had been, squirting its guns at him and he had not been dreaming! No, he had not been drinking. We the School's pilots, having incredibly established it was true report and not a leg-pull, viewed the Blenheim pilot's news with horror, dismay and not a little disquiet.

We thought we had overcome the enemy in being; the 'Rebellion' was over, and only a simple but effective clearing up action by our army on the ground was needed – or so we had believed. Now, the whole affair had taken on a completely new dimension. What one might class as a brave schoolboy's effort to suppress a local bully had suddenly become a full-scale grown-up's fight with flick-knives and knuckle-dusters - for which half-bricks and fisticuffs were totally inadequate.

What about these twin-engined, modern, German fighters? How many of them were there? Where did they come from? Where were they now? For what purpose had they arrived? The idea of sending any of my outdated aircraft out to be found by a modern, fast, well-armed monoplane firing cannon-shells sent shivers down my spine. A Gladiator could barely cruise to Mosul and back, and certainly not if he had to dogfight there as well. The prospect of meeting up with a 300mph, multi-cannon, Me110 when flying an unwieldy, 85mph Gordon-biplane was singularly unattractive. Or, for that matter, if one were to be piloting a plywood, unmanoeuvrable, twin-engined Oxford. The thought was appalling. 'Belling the Cat' was a kid's game in comparison.

Next day, 15 May, I decided it would be a good idea to go and learn where our relieving army force had got to. For safety's sake I would take a Gladiator, with another one flown by Flight Lieutenant Dicky Cleaver. We might perhaps be intercepted by an Iraqi machine, or even one of those German fighters. Either way we could if necessary give a good account of ourselves – and the second man could also provide a pin-point, for rescuers, if either of us had engine-failure over the arid desert.

We found Kingcol without difficulty. They were in the region of Rutbah Fort, stationary, well dispersed around the desert in wide open formation. We looked at them carefully. Most of the men waved, but no one seemed to make any signals with a meaning. So they appeared to be in good order – and the map showed they still had about 200 more miles to go. How long to get in? Well – our success against the Iraq Army had made us ridiculously optimistic. Any Iraqi opposition seemed to have completely evaporated. There was so little in fact that our searches for bodies of enemy troops to strafe were nearly always fruitless. Therefore they should have no fighting to delay them. Say, three to four days at a guess, before they would rolling past us and along the road to Baghdad – to take the formal surrender a day or two later? That, we judged, would be the probable course of events. It shows how little we knew about basic needs of a column on the ground!

Thirteen
The Luftwaffe In Mosul

One cannot but admire the German Luftwaffe for its capacity to overcome a mass of difficulties in getting their force to their destination – Mosul in Iraq.

To operate aircraft far from base requires strong engineering support, backed by a substantial supply of spares, tools and replacements – not to mention bombs and ammunition. Colonel Junck had managed, by impassioned pleading and doubtless some use of the Generals' names, to have had allotted to his force thirteen transport aircraft; ten of the work-horse three-engined Junkers 52s and three of the big four-engined Junkers 90s, to carry his non-aircrew personnel, bombs, ammunition, ground-support freight and equipment. But, to his acute distress, he found that his precious transports had been given the additional task of transporting Dr Grobba back to Baghdad for his liaison job with Raschid Ali.

Doktor Grobba by himself would not have been too bad, but that was far from all he required. Dr Grobba wanted – nay! – *insisted* on taking all his civilian staff, his files, his office equipment, his public-relations men, their cameramen, everybody's baggage… Also his intelligence staff, with *their* files, photographers, equipment, baggage – and goodness knows what else. By the time Dr Grobba had finished (and he had the backing of Hitler in person) there was far too little left for Junck.

Worse still, Junck was not allowed to keep and use all these transports later to build up his stocks. Ten of them had to return promptly to Greece, so as to be ready for the invasion of Crete within the next week. Only three of the Ju52s could remain, and they were not for general use; they each had special jobs to be done in Mosul.

Considering that they had had less than a week's notice, one can only stand amazed and admire the brilliance of the German detailed planning. The first Ju52 was fitted out as a radio station, equipped with powerful senders and receivers that could keep Junck in touch with any important headquarters, including the High Command in Berlin itself. The second was equipped as a chemical laboratory, with its own team of analysts. This was because the Iraqi fuel was of a very low 'octane-standard' and, by itself, it would have ruined the German aircraft engines. The team had at their disposal all the necessary gear for analysing the batches of fuel available locally, and to work out what dosage of chemical goodies would be needed to doctor it up to the required standard. The third aircraft with its separate team was, in effect, a little fuel-refinery. Their job was to measure out the quantities of chemicals from their stocks on board, add them to the Iraqi fuel, mix them in – and ensure that the aircraft fuel-tanks were supplied with the correctly modified result – till the stocks ran out.

Moving the operational aircraft was equally well thought through – yet fraught with problems. Having myself been an organiser and pilot with the task of moving aircraft from one distant country, through an area with meagre facilities, to another, my heart bleeds for Colonel Junck. After attempts to ensure Turkey's co-operation had failed, his aircraft and support-force had to stage the long way round through Athens. Greece had recently fallen to the Germans, but though the greater part of their task was simply conceived it proved much more difficult to deliver. It must be borne in mind, too, that none of the pilots had ever operated their aircraft in the area before. Everything was new to them and, from my own wartime knowledge, support-facilities were sketchy.

The first leg was 250 miles over the sea from Athens to the island of Rhodes. The flight was by day and, for security reasons, wireless-silence would have been rigid. However, the good visibility and the mass of islands around there would make map-reading comparatively simple even for a fairly inexperienced leader. A brief rest followed, before pressing onwards. The next leg was less pleasant. It was Rhodes to Damascus – 500 miles, again all over the sea and this time it was by night.

Damascus, in Syria, answered at that time to the Vichy French. As we know, Admiral Darlan, elected Vice-Premier of France, had promised in Paris that Damascus would provide the necessary facilities for staging through to Mosul. Political promises are not always honoured, however, as in this case – the French High Commissioner in Syria claimed never to have heard what Darlan or anybody else in Paris had said upon this subject. Anyway, he was the man on the spot and alleged promises from Paris cut no ice with him. He had to think, he cried vociferously, of bombing raids by the British, should they perchance get to hear that German aircraft were there. So, when the first flights of aircraft arrived under command of Lieutenant Woerner – five He111 bombers and three Me110 fighters – they were refused fuel by the French commandant of the airfield. He was supported in this by the German *Chargé d'Affaires*, Dr Rahn, who required from them that they should stage through Palmyra – and not Damascus. In the afternoon they pressed on again. First they went the 150 miles to Palmyra to ensure adequate arrangements for all the other aircraft which were to follow, and then continued the final 250 miles to Mosul, to get combat-ready.

It was by any standards a fine effort – and especially by a formation leader who was only a lieutenant. After reaching Athens from their various start-points, they had then done 4 stages totalling about 1,200 miles in 36 hours, most of it over the sea or barren desert, under wireless-silence. They had been messed about in Damascus by 2 French figure-heads and a German civilian. Yet, they arrived in Mosul on 13 May, only 1 week after Junck had reported to Berlin for his original briefing. Speaking from personal experience, they must have all been very tired. It was a superb performance, particularly as lieutenants do not normally carry much weight, or experience.

Next day, 14 May, the transports were coming through to Mosul and discharging their loads. They had staged a different route to the bombers and fighters, to the north, via Aleppo. All the German personnel found the Mosul accommodation, which had been built to British standards about fifteen years earlier, very comfortable though not cool during the scorching daylight hours when a thermometer in the shade would be teetering round the 110-115°F mark. The trees, grass and flower-beds which had grown up helped to make it pleasanter.

Captain Schwanhauser also arrived with three more He111s and three Me110s. He had started with five bombers, heavily overloaded with spares and equipment for use by the detachment in Mosul. This equipment could not be carried on the transports because Dr Grobba's load had already claimed the space. Palmyra was a much less well cared-for airfield than Damascus. It was very rough, and this had caused the tail wheels on two of them to collapse. They had to be left behind for repair. As luck would have it three British fighters appeared overhead from out of nowhere, saw the Germans, dived down and shot them up as they sat there, stuck fast and helpless.

On 15 May, Colonel Junck himself arrived with nine more aircraft. He had come through Palmyra and seen his two damaged Heinkels, effectively snatched away from his all-too-small strength of bombers. As he saw it, there had been no real operational necessity for the switch. It was caused by a couple of chicken-hearted French officials, backed up by a German civilian member of the political staff – all of whom probably had no aviation knowledge anyway and were scared of a chance bomb! He must have been absolutely hopping mad at what they had cost him and his operational effort. That was by no means the last of a raft of difficulties for him, both operational and administrative.

He knew from German sources that Kingcol was on its way towards Habbaniya, and he believed it had taken Rutbah on 11 May, thus leaving only 200 miles more to go – and that was four days earlier. This estimate was in fact untrue for Kingcol did not leave Nathanya on the Mediterranean coast until the 11th. It must have been Glubb and his Bedouin Arab Auxiliaries, skirmishing 400 miles ahead of the main body. They stayed at Rutbah and the column did not meet up with them till 14 May. Nevertheless, Junck appreciated quite correctly that if Kingcol were to reach Habbaniya, the ensuing problems in capturing that complex and eliminating the British in Iraq would be immense. Although he had only just arrived, he immediately sent off a He111 bomber to find out where Kingcol really was, to do it any damage that could be managed, and to bring back the facts.

The pilot duly found Kingcol at Rutbah, dropped a few bombs and went home to Mosul. As the entire column was dispersed around the desert in wide formation, the bombs did no particular damage and no trouble was caused.

The members of Kingcol, on the ground, saw the Heinkel flying around fairly high up and easily recognisable from its unique oval-shaped wings. Lower, obviously looking down at their vehicles and trying to identify any signals being made, they could also see two Gladiator fighters with British markings. Soon the Gladiators flew off in the direction of Habbaniya. The Heinkel later dropped its ineffectual bombs, and flew off in the direction of Mosul. Clearly, to the fury of the soldiers on the ground who could plainly see all three aircraft above them, none of the pilots had noticed his enemy.

Oddly enough, that curious story is sound for there is a very remarkable thing about flying an aircraft. All too often, both inside and outside the cockpit, you don't see something unless you are at least half-expecting to see it. The fighter pilots on that day 'knew' from the Fighter-Blenheim pilot's story that there were only fighters in Iraq. Moreover, they also 'knew' full-well that no German fighter would be daft enough to be swanning about over an empty desert, hundreds of miles from anywhere, in the vicinity of Rutbah oil-pumping station. If any Me110 fighter was sniffing for trade anywhere, it would be to pick up some unsuspecting machine by sneaking around Habbaniya. Germans at Rutbah? Ridiculous! So the Heinkel flew away unobserved.

The tale maddens me, for I was leader of the Gladiators. Dicky and I missed a golden opportunity just because we were mentally numb and dumb. I would dearly have loved to take a squirt at the Heinkel.

One of the officers who had arrived in Mosul was Major Axel von Blomberg, son of *Feldmarschall* von Blomberg, Hitler's Minister of War until he was sacked for taking as his second wife a young lady who was reputedly a prostitute. He was due to become head of the German Military Mission, to be set up as soon as possible, working alongside Dr Grobba. Colonel Junck sent him across in a He111 to Raschid airfield in Baghdad to make arrangements for a council of war next morning, 16 May, which would include Grobba and the Iraqi authorities. Von Blomberg asked that his pilot should fly low across the city, particularly over the bridges where they knew Iraqi troops were on guard-duty, so as to 'show-the-flag' for them, to give their morale a boost and to demonstrate publicly that their German allies were actually on hand and already operating in the country.

As they flew over the guarded main bridge into the city from the west, an Iraqi machine-gunner, not recognising the aircraft's shape and therefore believing it was an enemy machine, Iraqi markings or no, shot at it. It was low enough for him to hit it with several bullets. When it landed at Raschid airfield Major von Blomberg was still sitting in his seat, but with a bullet through his neck, quite dead. The Iraqi broadcasts claimed that the bullet came from a wandering tribesman, loose around the city with his rifle; he had taken pot-shots at the Heinkel, and the accident was deeply regretted. What else *could* they say?

At the end of the day, 15 May, Junck counted heads and tails. He had, ready for combat, five He111 bombers, twelve Me110 fighters, a communications flight with a light aircraft, a section of anti-aircraft cannon and, of course, his radio station, his chemical laboratory and his fuel refinery in the three Ju52s.

Later, he was to get some replacement aircraft for those he lost, but it never really came up to a strength commensurate with his task.

Next morning, Junck went across to Baghdad for his first joint conference. It was attended by Dr Grobba, Raschid Ali, the Iraqi President, his War Minister and a representative of the Iraqi Air Force. After a lot of discussion, they decided on a priority list for the tasks to be undertaken. It was a straight statement of what needed to be done; it contained no helpful information spelling out how his objectives were supposed to be achieved. The priority list was:

First Priority
To repel the British land forces – Kingcol – who were coming to succour Habbaniya and who by that date were only about 50 miles away.

Second Priority
To capture Habbaniya itself – it was tacitly assumed that the Iraqi Army would make the actual assault.

Overall
Maximum effort was required from the Luftwaffe to encourage the Iraqis. The wording the Germans used in their version was 'spine straightening' for the Iraqis, whose entire army had become terrified of bombing by British aircraft.

In fact, Junck's task, as dictated to him by Grobba and Raschid Ali was already impossible and far and away beyond the 'Heroic Gesture' which he had been sent to make. The rout by the Flying Training School, between 2 and 6 May, of the Iraqi Army and Air Force had so shattered their morale that they never appeared again to attack or defend in any degree of force. Moreover, when Kingcol eventually arrived on its rescue mission from Palestine, it encamped itself comfortably around Habbaniya, without having even seen a single Iraqi soldier on the way there.

Junck decided that, as there was no chance of his few aircraft making a significant dent in the progress of an army column dispersed across miles of desert, he would make an attack on Habbaniya that same afternoon, 16 May. After all, maximum effort had been asked from the Luftwaffe. He would do his best.

Fourteen
Clearing Up: Days 16-18

16 May began as a special day for me. The hospital was not hard-pressed, now that there was virtually no fighting, and I had used our peace-time break to good effect. Not only had I had time to contact and chat-up one of the nursing sisters, but she had graciously agreed to join me for a swim and maybe a cup of tea or a drink afterwards. We were sitting in the shade of the mess veranda, having a long, cold soft drink and hoping to cool off a bit before going over to the pool – the water there got so warm it was like bathing in soup.

I was an object of deep envy, having a girl to talk to. My colleagues found innumerable reasons to come by and pass the time of day. High overhead, the protecting Gladiator patrolled comfortably, backwards and forwards at minimum throttle to save fuel, criss-crossing the blue sky above us. I believed it to be Dicky Cleaver up on patrol, but I wasn't certain. Up there too, but not nearly so high, was a second aircraft, one of John Hawtrey's Audaxes doing a wireless test. It was something to do with providing air-to-ground contact with Kingcol, to use when it arrived near our doorstep. Once it had arrived, we were sure that the Iraqi Army would not dare to attack again. Wonderful! Added to that, we now knew for sure that the column was only a few days away. At last we had sure knowledge of its progress, acquired only the day before when Dicky and I in our Gladiators had actually seen it. Life was getting better and better by the hour. We should be safe once more and life could continue peacefully, like this afternoon. Perhaps I could, with luck, even consolidate my opening gambit with the nursing sister? In this peaceful situation, I could have a very good try.

Suddenly, there was the noise of aircraft-engines that I had never heard before. Then the noise of cannon-shells being fired, and exploding in the camp. They were not around us on the mess lawn, which was one good point, but unluckily they seemed to be well placed among our parked aircraft on the airfield and the polo-pitch. I picked the aircraft out at once. There were six Me110 fighters, strafing us with their multiple-cannon. As I watched, one of them peeled off and swung towards the Audax, up there, its pilot placidly driving round and round while the radio-operator had his head down in the back, concentrating on his tests.

The Audax pilot cannot have seen the Messerschmitt coming. I could see flashes from the muzzles of the fighter's cannon and, almost instantly, corresponding flashes on the Audax as the shells burst. Then, some seconds later, the sounds reached us on the lawn as the Audax heeled over crazily and swung down towards the ground below. In total impotence I swore brutally at the fighter. Then, imploringly, to the Audax pilot, 'Pull out, pull her out – pull out for God's sake! Pull out *now*, or bale out before you're too low – PLEASE!' Slowly, all too slowly, he did pull out and plainly he was not aiming for the polo-pitch. He was going for the main airfield, and the extra space it gave him.

I was up and running for the airfield, yelling over my shoulder, 'Sorry Sister!' And then following it with the afterthought, 'Get an ambulance at once.' More stupidity on my part – she never heard me – a true and efficient professional, she was already up and running flat out for the mess telephone.

The pilot, dead or alive, would of course be down somewhere long before I could ever get near him, but what stopped me in my tracks before I had done fifty yards was a sound of strange engines, again. I looked up, in case I needed somehow to find some cover. To my total incredulity I saw the impossible. Three German aircraft at about 6,000ft, with the unmistakable curved planform of wings which proclaimed them as Heinkel 111 *bombers*! Still, today, I remember clearly the thoughts flashing through my mind; 'It can't be true! They haven't the range. They couldn't get here. What the hell goes on?'

Well, what went on was some very good bombing. I can imagine, now, that the young German fighter pilots did not distinguish between two somewhat similar elderly biplanes and in all likelihood reckoned they had shot down our Gladiator protective-patrol. What else would have been up there, merely stooging around? Then they could well have radioed back their success in shooting down the aircraft and clearing the air. True or not, the Heinkels took plenty of time over their job.

There is a cardinal rule for attacking ground-targets:

Try to achieve surprise. Then, make one flashing flyby attack – hit or miss – and AWAY! If you ever come back for another go, the defences have been aroused, and they are angry. The hornets nest you have stirred up will get you for sure on the second time around.

The Heinkels made two passes, dropping six bombs on each run, two from each Heinkel. They hit their targets fair and square. They went for the hangars which, normally, are the most productive airfield targets; the ensuing fierce petrol-fires inside do great damage. Naturally, the biggest hangars are the juiciest.

Looking up, I could clearly see our patrolling Gladiator diving down from high above in time for an attack during the second bombing-run. He pressed home to point-blank range and, when it reached us, the tearing-calico sound of his four front guns was clear and crisp. Full of courage, he seemed to hang there as on a string while his burst of fire went on and on till his ammunition must have been exhausted – it felt like an age. I couldn't distinguish the sound of the He111 rear-gunners, though they must have been firing back.

Suddenly, the fighter nosed down slightly and I thought 'Good; he's breaking off the engagement.' I could see one of the He111s streaming white vapour behind it as they too broke off their attack. I muttered, 'Great! Dicky's got him! I hope that's fuel coming out and, with luck, the sod'll catch fire!'

I glanced back to the fighter. He was continuing steadily downwards, wings quite level, but showing no signs of turning away. He didn't turn. He went on, down and down, until he went smack into the desert. A bit later we went out to collect his remains. There was not a lot left, but enough to see that he hadn't been Dicky Cleaver. He was Flying Officer G.D.F. Herrtage, of 94 Squadron, who had come from Egypt with his Gladiator to help us out. The Heinkel rear-gunners had shot him stone dead. He got his bird, however, because we later found the bomber, crash-landed, wheels-up, beside the Haditha road en route to Mosul. We supposed its crew had been collected safely for of them there was no sign.

Meanwhile, I walked down to the airfield, knowing there would be nothing I could do to help the Audax crew by the time I got there. The machine was depressingly crashed and mangled but more or less in one lump. The pilot though gravely wounded had been found alive, barely. He had already been cut free and rushed off to hospital. His flying controls had been shot to bits and he had done a magnificent job nursing it down at all. The wireless-operator had been hit by an explosive cannon-shell coming through the fabric fuselage-covering. He was very messily dead.

I wondered how the aircraft-maintenance and workshops hangars had fared. They were the largest, so the Germans had concentrated on them. They had made a very good bombing-job indeed, doing a lot of damage and they killed several people. Our only piece of good luck, and that was very slight, was that their main achievement was to damage further the already damaged aircraft under repair – and not the few flyable ones that we were still using.

The engineer-officer in charge of all the work down there – now the rubbish down there – was a wing commander. He was among the finest of the old-school craftsmen in the Air Force. Admittedly, he tended to keep himself rather tied down by the rules in the books – thereby infuriating Larry Ling when we had proposed making some original do-it-yourself changes to his precious Oxfords. Nevertheless, he had been performing miracles on our machines during the plateau affair and immediately afterwards. If human ingenuity and unremitting effort could make it fly, it was achieved. And, as any engineer of the old school would do after he said a pilot could fly one of his repair jobs, he would always want to come up on air-test in the back seat with the pilot – any pilot, even the most junior and inexperienced ones – to prove he really believed in the quality of his work. The only exception was if the machine was a single-seater-fighter. He had become very crusty and soured while our panic battle was in progress, because I spared no time to make test flights in the Oxfords. I took our flying colanders as they stood and flatly refused to let him come up with us, at any time. Mistakenly, in spite of my assurances, he had taken my veto as gravely reflecting my mistrust in his work. Of course, the opposite was the case – it was he whom I was trying to preserve as best I could. His work was essential and irreplaceable. He was a charming individual and I valued him as a friend, even though he was twenty years older than me.

During our 'peace-time' break, shortly after the plateau affair and before we heard about any Germans, I had been drinking with him in the mess one evening. He was in a black mood and even after a good many noggins he had not snapped out of it. I found the courage to pry into his private thoughts – I was not very tactful, but I too had had a few slugs. I wanted him to snap out of his sadness, to help him catch up with and enjoy one of those all-too-rare pleasant evenings we had been missing lately.

He looked long and deep into his tankard before answering. 'I reckon,' he said, 'that I'm unlucky. In the First World War, when I was abroad, some bastard put my wife in a family way. Now, in this flaming war, here I am, stuck on my own in this misbegotten country – and some new bastard has gone and put my daughter in a family way.' He took another swig of ale, and shook his head.

He was right; he *was* an unlucky fellow. A few days after our conversation he was in the hangars working his heart out for us fliers. Then the He111s blasted them – and blew him to bits.

17 May, the day after the Messerschmitts' and the Heinkels' visit, turned out to be a red-letter day for us. We stopped feeling like the poor relations of the Middle East. Unannounced, in the morning and more than welcome, four more Gladiators of 94 Squadron and half-a-dozen Blenheim bombers from two flights of 84 Squadron arrived from their bases in the Mediterranean area. But, best of all, they all had their pilots with them. We could now swing from striving just to keep our enemies on the bottom-end of the see-saw, right over to out-and-out attack, particularly against those unwelcome Germans.

On the other side of the coin, the Wellingtons commanded by my friend Tommy Rivett-Carnac were being withdrawn from Basrah, which was regrettable for us. Although we had not seen them over Habbaniya since that first day's horrendous attack against the plateau, they had been night bombing targets all around Baghdad, keeping up the relentless pressure. Now they were reserved for badly needed raids on the Libyan ports (to try and hamstring Rommel in the Western Desert) and for attacks on the German airfields in Greece. However, we felt that with our invaluable reinforcements we had won much more on the deal than we were losing.

That was not by any means all. The day before Heinkel-day we had also received, from Aboukir in Egypt, two of the special long-range Hurricane IICs. These fighters had cannons instead of machine-guns, and extra tankage fitted to give them a range and fighting capacity far beyond the normal models. What better use could there now be for them other than to pay Mosul a visit?

So, that same afternoon, 17th, they and our Blenheim fighters returned the compliment. It was 200 miles each way, and they made the trip at very low level, doing the simplest kind of navigation – following the road. To be accurate, not really a road, but a number of tracks across the desert, first to Haditha and then bearing right for Mosul. It was simple, but by no means stupid. First, flying on your own with no radio surveillance over 200 miles of featureless desert, it is dead easy to get lost. Second, being right down on the ground, there was less chance of being seen from above, and no one below on those meandering tracks would be able to pass the word on ahead.

In any case, a really low cross-country flight is a wonderful experience. It is the only time one can get the feeling of an aeroplane's terrific speed. The ground streaks past under the wings unbelievably fast. Different coloured patches of sand flow by; it's like running your hand across a patchwork quilt. You lift your machine gently upwards to clear hummocks, and then ease her down again the other side to stay low, low, low.

As one approaches the target, the adrenaline starts to pump, giving a tingling sensation between the shoulder-blades, and maybe some sweat trickles down. Final checks. Bombs – 'fused'. Guns – safety-catches 'off'. All set. The landmarks signifying the target appear ahead; in this case, dusty-green trees near the airfield, and some houses, sticking up out of the yellow sand. Will the enemy react?

Then the attack – utterly absorbing, total concentration – not an atom of space in your conscious mind for fear. You have no time to think about yourself.

Next, if you have not been badly hit, more concentration on the task of getting away and back home, safely. Bomber-boys used to say that up to the instant of bomb-release, you were working for your King and Country; when you heard the words 'Bombs Gone!' you began to work for your wife and family.

When they returned, our force reported that they had burned one Heinkel, blown up a Messerschmitt and damaged four other aircraft, including a Ju52 transport. One Hurricane did not return because, it was believed, he had flown into the fragments of his exploding Me110.

The pilot of that missing Hurricane was Flight Lieutenant Sir Roderic MacRobert of 94 Squadron. He was the third and last of three brothers to lose his life flying; two in the war and one in a 1938 accident. Their mother, Lady MacRobert, paid for and presented three Hurricanes to the RAF for use in the Middle East, each bearing the family crest and the name of one of her sons. Later she also presented a Stirling bomber to the Air Force, named 'MacRobert's Reply'.

The successful attack on Mosul was not the only good news on that splendid day. We had sent a couple of our newly arrived 'Gladiators-with-pilots' to look for trade by patrolling over Raschid airfield at Baghdad. The pilots were Sergeants L.E. Smith and W.H. Dunwoodie, also of 94 Squadron. What should they see upon arrival there but two Me110s taxying out to take off! With cries of joy and showing far more enthusiasm than skill, they dived down to attack. In their excitement their dive was far too steep; they overshot and missed the Me110s completely.

Then, an incredible thing happened. The far faster twin-engined monoplane fighters did not just fly away, as they could have done. They turned back and attempted to dog-fight with the slower, single-engined, and extremely manoeuvrable Gladiator biplanes. Added to that, as our cock-a-hoop pilots reported during de-briefing later, they apparently had no rear-gunners for there was no return fire from the rear-firing gun position. Absence of gunfire was curious, but most welcome. If a twin-engined and comparatively sluggish monoplane cares to dog-fight, using front-guns only against an efficient and agile biplane, let it – both Me110s were promptly shot down in flames.

Their success was celebrated enthusiastically. We were absolutely delighted at the competent and effective victory in the air over the two Messerschmitt fighters. We should have been ecstatic had we known the real truth. Our good fortune went far beyond a satisfying win by our meagre and ill-equipped force. We had at that time no knowledge of Raschid Ali's master plan to oust the British from Iraq with Axis help – nor how far he had gone and how nearly he had succeeded. Nor did we have any idea that, only the day before, a new master list of German-Iraqi priorities had been drawn up, and that capture of Habbaniya was the key element. Our mistaken impression was that our struggle remained, essentially, one of suppressing a local Iraqi rebellion. We imagined that the Germans had adroitly grabbed the chance to send over a few aircraft in order to capitalise on any advantage which might accrue to them.

It is inconceivable that, with Kingcol bearing down upon Habbaniya, new detailed joint plans to prevent its arrival would not have been put in hand at once. The absence of gunfire from the rear seats of the Me110 fighters is a powerful indication that Junck had sent his planning officers to Baghdad, in place of the rear-gunners. On top of that, and unknown to us at the time, the designate head of the German Military Mission to Iraq, Major von Blomberg had already been killed; indeed, when we heard of Blomberg's death, we naturally assumed he must have been in one of the fighters. For the Germans, the end result of those two tragedies was that, by the time the ensuing confusion had been sorted out, it was far too late to recover the ground that had been lost.

It is reasonable to judge that, after the defeat of the forces on the plateau and the resulting want of courage which had spread throughout the Iraq Army, this little air-victory against the German Luftwaffe was the second major turning point of our campaign.

Fifteen
Clearing Up: Days 19-31

The Army's stories of their advance from the Mediterranean to Baghdad, the Iraqi surrender, the liberation of the Embassy and the subsequent assumption of control are brilliantly told by Somerset de Chair in his book *The Golden Carpet*. He was the Intelligence Officer and keeper of the War Diary for Kingcol. His official records are in the Army archives. The Army story is not mine, for here I try only to record – as accurately as possible – what we saw from our side of the fence, at that time. Bear in mind also that, in early 1941, the RAF did not yet fully appreciate its khaki-uniformed colleagues.

It is curious to reflect on just how little the majority of RAF pilots understood the Army's problems and ways of working in those days. It is fair to say too that the same applied in the reverse direction. Certainly it was so with us in Habbaniya. We, the pilots, were convinced that the School, with a few air-reinforcements, had already both defeated the Iraqi ground and air forces and virtually destroyed their morale. All that would be needed therefore from Kingcol, when it eventually arrived (as we saw it) would be to march straight on to Baghdad and accept Raschid Ali's surrender. In hindsight, this was an over-simplification, and very unreasonable.

Our knowledge of the magnitude of the Iraqi defeat had not reached Kingcol. So when they proceeded prudently and gently; our RAF view was one of frustration at the (apparent) lack of urgency and desire to profit from our earlier and hard-won successes. Communication with the ground forces was not my business, but we found it remarkable to learn later of the apparent inadequacy and uselessness of the intelligence which was used by our would-be rescuers. They had little idea as to how we were faring, what we had already done and even less as to what, where and how was their enemy? Perhaps it resulted from the sentiments of the Brigade Major, Sir Peter Grant-Lawson – Somerset de Chair, Intelligence Officer and keeper of the column's official diary, records Sir Peter saying to him, bluntly: 'Intelligence doesn't matter a shit.' Maybe it was because they mistrusted the RAF's views upon the ground-forces' task ahead? Or perhaps it was something to do with the attitude of the CO, Brigadier Joe Kingstone – Somerset writes that the Brigadier said to him: 'Don't you worry about the enemy – we'll find out all about him when we run into him.'

Whatever the reason, the column, approaching Habbaniya from the Rutbah side, carefully made a big detour to the south and west, right round the other side of the lake. It might have been partly to do with flooding from Iraqi-breached dikes near the river but, certainly, they wished to be sure they did not get nipped in the gap between our camp and any Iraqis still holding on to the plateau. De Chair wrote that he raced ahead, eager to catch a first glimpse of their objective. As he came over the lip of the plateau he could suddenly see it all spread out before him. Soon, he was driving along smooth tarmac roads, between flowering oleanders and bougainvillaea. He said it was hard to accept that the spearpoint of the relieving column was about to enter a besieged settlement. So far as we were concerned, the term 'besieged settlement' was laughable. No Iraqi soldier had been seen for twelve days and the so-called 'siege' was past history.

It must have been very irritating and frustrating for them to find that, after slogging determinedly across 450 miles of barren and difficult country, the dicey rescue they had been sent to achieve was by then totally unnecessary. Twelve days earlier, before the column had even set out, we had filled the Iraqi Army with such dread of RAF attack that Kingcol reached Habbaniya on 18 May having met no opposition whatsoever except for the bombs dropped by the Luftwaffe. Their most taxing problem had been to get 500 vehicles over the soft sand and flooded areas immediately west of Habbaniya. There was not one single 'besieging' Iraqi soldier to be seen, anywhere.

All was not wasted. De Chair adds light-heartedly that, as he drove towards civilisation, a great desire welled up in him – to get a hot bath, even if he had to break into every building in the camp to find one. Luckily, he did not have to destroy one single building in order to satisfy his dearest wish.

On their way across the desert from Rutbah, Junck had been doing his best over the previous two days with his limited forces to comply with priority one in the joint German-Iraqi plans – to stop Kingcol relieving Habbaniya. His aircraft had dropped bombs and done some strafing with their cannon. They had caused some damage and a few casualties. In particular they had instilled fear into Glubb's Bedouin Arab Auxiliaries who had not met this kind of warfare before. But, as for Junck's forces by themselves, stopping the column's steady advance towards its objective had naturally been a hopeless brief.

We had no means of telling so, but the balance of advantage from these fruitless attacks was heavily in our favour. They had done comparatively little damage and had no adverse effect on Kingcol's advance. On the other hand, they were cutting deeply into Junck's meagre war-supplies. He was running short of bombs. His belts of cannon-shells needed re-stocking. The dust-laden atmosphere was playing havoc with the serviceability of his machines. He had no special sand-filters and the grains of silicone were wearing away the pistons and bearings of the engines at dreadful speed. Junck begged his masters to supply him with tropicalised aircraft, equipped to cope with sand, but none were forthcoming. He asked for more bombs, and they did not arrive. They tried to get a ship load of correct-octane fuel brought in through Beirut, but failed.

We, the pilot-spearhead at Habbaniya fondly imagined that the column of troops called Kingcol was a force meant first to rescue us and then, when that job was over, promptly to rush on to Baghdad and take the surrender. Not a bit of it. It was merely a flying column ordered to come as quickly as possible and save our bacon, holding the besieging Iraqis at bay until the main force caught up and finished the job. Main force? What 'main force'? We now learned it was called 'Habforce' and it was commanded by Major-General J.G.W. Clark, MC, whose headquarters was still a long way back, near an oil-pumping station, named H.4, on the Haifa-Kirkuk pipeline. We had to wait.

To our great disappointment and frustration Kingcol ensconced itself safely in camp by Habbaniya lake, where they were in easy reach of our facilities. They could bathe in the clear water after their epic eight-day trans-desert rush in scarifying heat and dust – they had had no water except that which they carried for cooking and drinking. No shaving, even. Brigadier Kingcome always shared whatever hardships there might be with his men. This was his normal practice. He too pitched his tent out by the lake, with a swim nearby. On 18 May General Clark was flown in by Blenheim from his headquarters at H.4 on the pipeline. He moved immediately into the most comfortable quarters he could find, which was the AOC's Residence, Air House. It had been empty since Air Vice-Marshal Smart and then Lady Holman had left it, nearly three weeks before. It was a comfortable white villa, luxuriously appointed. Electric fans moved the hot and sometimes dusty air. Soft Persian carpets deadened the stamp of military boots and shoes. There he awaited the arrival of his troops. This was *his* normal practice.

Air Vice-Marshal John D'Albiac also flew in on 18 May, to take Smart's place as AOC. He had come from Greece via Egypt. He also moved into Air House.

Thanks to Kingcol, we were able to go over to a limited offensive on the ground, as well as in the air. Their first objective had to be the bridge over the Euphrates river at Fallujah. It was the only bridge for crossing the Euphrates on the way to Baghdad. Our intelligence said it was held by about 1,000 Iraqi troops who were in touch with Baghdad by telephone and radio.

The general plan, we were told, was to start the following night, 19 May, by putting about 1,500 of our troops around Fallujah village under cover of darkness, on both sides of the river. Then, at first light, the School would produce one of its 'blitz' attacks and go on for about an hour. Pamphlets would then be dropped, inviting the garrison to surrender. If after thirty minutes grace they had not hoisted a white flag, the School's blitz would begin again, and go on all day. If the Iraqis had not surrendered by 6 p.m., the army would withdraw back into camp and a new plan would be thought out. They did not plan to advance and capture the bridge.

What was this 'Come back into camp if the enemy had not *surrendered* by 6 p.m.?' We, the seasoned and hardened pilots of the plateau-days, thought this last idea was too mimsy and flimsy for words. No one bothered to explain to us that it was not because they were chicken – it was because flooding from the dikes which the Iraqis had breached prevented any serious ground-attack.

The detailed attack-plan took account of the fact (known by the Army but not the RAF) that the Iraqis had an army of which the force so far unused was at least 40,000 men, with tanks. They might react, and Kingcol had no armour. Therefore an initial element of the Army plan was to have the Air Force sever the enemy's communication-links with Baghdad, and stop them calling for air-support or ground reinforcements.

When the very first shafts of light crossed the dawn sky next morning our Audax dive-bombers came in, pin-pointed their radio-station and, with Dead-Eyed-Dick accuracy, flattened it. Two separate sets of telephone lines remained, still needing attention.

The first set had only a few wires, but they stretched across the cultivation and a nearby landing was quite impossible. They were, however, neatly dealt with by one of the Audaxes which flew backwards and forwards between the poles for about a mile. He then returned to have the telephone wires, which had been wound around his machine by the propeller, removed and the minor damage was fixed up.

The second set had many wires, running across the desert behind Fallujah village. They were too much of an obstruction to be cut by a flying aeroplane without serious risk of a crash. So, another Audax landed on the desert and taxied up between two poles, leaving the engine running. The gunner stood guard, with his rear-mounted machine-gun, to keep unfriendly strangers at a discreet distance. The pilot then climbed up on to the top wing and cut all the wires with a large pair of shears which he had prudently brought with him. He said the thing he was most scared of was the thought of slipping and falling off the wing, to be chopped up by the spinning propeller.

No strangers or spectators were to be seen anywhere, so the pilot took over the task of manning the rear-gun. This was to let the gunner also have his fair share of the amusements. They had brought an axe with them, so the gunner got out and chopped down two telegraph poles. Then they got back into the aircraft, took off again, and flew home.

Meanwhile, Valentias had flown up from Basrah, timed to arrive immediately after the communications had been cut. They unloaded soldiers who took up their positions behind the village. The Valentias took off again and went home. Then the School started its 'blitz' attack.

It was just like going back to the old days over the plateau, but with hardly any returning ground-fire. We used every available aircraft, not stopping engines between sorties – bomb, scoot back, re-load, return, bomb, and so on.

By this time all our Audax and Gordon dive-bombers were becoming breath-takingly precise with their attacks. A water tower is a very small target, but one of the Gordons hit it with two successive 250lb bombs. Such remarkable accuracy might have occurred because they were going right down and pulling out *extremely* low! I was pattern-bombing with my clutch of Oxfords, and carrying an automatic camera that was pointing downwards to record the results. As usual, for maximum accuracy, we were only at 1,000ft. That did not prevent one of my prints showing my bombs falling and, well below them, an Audax pulling out of its dive.

Our army reported back that the Iraqis were well positioned and returning spirited and extremely effective ground-fire, thus producing sound and tough ground-defence. We dropped the pamphlets. After half-an-hour there was no surrender so the attacks went on all the morning. By late morning there seemed to be very little movement of any sort and by 1 p.m. there was nothing at all for us to see from above. We told the army so, and invited them in to capture the bridge. Politely, they declined, suggesting that it might be a trap, and anyway their troops were totally untrained for street-fighting. This was very irritating.

Flight Lieutenant Dan Cremin, in discussion with John Hawtrey, decided that matters were so quiet he would go to have a close look. He flew round, over, back and forth across the village, going down well below a hundred feet. Nothing. No gun-fire. No soldiers. Not even any civilians. Zilch. It was a dead city. The defence seemed suddenly to have evaporated completely. The school, having already made over 100 sorties, called halt.

The army got ready. At 2 p.m., under cover of a co-ordinated pattern and dive-bombing attack, the army rushed the bridge in case the enemy might try to blow it up. Not only was there no resistance, there was no enemy. The whole place appeared to be completely deserted. But where could they have vanished? They certainly had not escaped, for our forces were on all sides. Finally, a careful search produced 26 officers (including a General) and 300 soldiers, found sheltering in the village hospital.

Interrogation afterwards revealed the explanation for the shift from spirited defence to surrender within an hour. It stemmed from an experience of the previous year. The Iraqi Army and Air Force were largely British trained. Not only were a cadre of Iraqi officers and pilots trained in Britain but there were a small number of British officers, in Baghdad, attached to them for helping with exercises and training on the spot. In 1940, the annual exercise-manoeuvre for the Iraqi Staff College was 'The defence of Fallujah Bridge against ground attack.' The British staff had planned the defence magnificently and indeed when played in real life it was superb, so far as it went. And, where it went was 12.30. Being an exercise, it stopped at lunchtime. For the unfortunate Iraqis who were playing the exercise for real, in 1941, there had been no scenario for them to follow after the lunch interval!

The School had made 134 sorties and dropped $9\frac{1}{4}$ tons of bombs. There were no Army or Air Force casualties. It was very satisfying to learn also that the prisoners interrogated said the morale of the whole entire Iraqi Army, everywhere, was at rock bottom. Our prisoners insisted that their army feared our intensive air-attacks greatly. Clearly, tales from the plateau had magnified themselves in each telling. This reinforced the School's earlier suspicion that Iraqi resistance would be minimal – but of which we had had no confirmation so far from the other side.

By late afternoon, we in the School were jubilant beyond belief. On 20 May we knew that, solely by the use of our aircraft, we had beaten Iraqi ground forces for a second time and the whole Iraqi Army had come to dread our attacks. Now, we felt, heigh-ho for Kingcol and Baghdad, streaming forwards against negligible opposition all the way, and any snags which might arise could easily be coped with. Finally, there would be an enforced truce to bring it all to an end. Victory was in sight.

Our wild hopes were crushed. The Army powers-that-be in the form of General Clark thought otherwise. He decided they would stay precisely where they were – on the edge of Lake Habbaniya, comfortably ensconced and happily bathing. This, we learned, was to let the other parts of Habforce catch up from H.4.

We were deeply disappointed at the time and furious that our efforts were, we feared, being frittered away. We believed that Iraqi Army morale, right then, was at rock bottom. Right or wrong, we felt that our army was not cashing in on the advantages we had presented to them on a plate. We were wrong. Clark knew, and we did not, that the remaining 40,000 Iraqi troops had plenty of armour, and we had none. With that advantage in armour, a reasonably determined bunch of Iraqi girl-scouts could have mopped up Habforce.

It did not matter in the end. We had got our troops across the bridge and on the same side of the Euphrates as the city of Baghdad. Some resistance remained, but serious defence or defiance from the Iraqis had more or less evaporated. The Germans, lacking the Iraqi support with 'stiffened-spines' that they needed so desperately, saw their efforts and aircraft becoming less and less effective. Only isolated incidents could follow.

Next morning while our army pulled itself together, we managed to get on the line nine Oxfords, fourteen Audaxes, five Gordons, and four Blenheims of 84 Squadron. We attacked Raschid airfield in Baghdad. We had a screen of no less than thirteen Gladiators around and above us. It felt marvellous. To fighters' disappointment and bombers' relief, no German aircraft turned up. The leading Oxford (not me) carried the camera and the photographs taken showed excellent results.

I chose to lead the Gordon formation of five, treating myself to some low dive-bombing which is the greatest fun – when you compare it to the intense but tame concentration needed to fly accurately for the high-and-level stuff. On the way home we flew over the desert, really low down. 'Really low' in that context meant with the wheels about six or less feet above the sand, lifting up slightly every so often to clear little black camel-thorn bushes and trees, and then going down again the other side. Below, in the blinding, scorching sunlight, our jet-black shadows raced along over the desert beneath us.

Black shadows like that always stand out starkly and, usually, when you see one from above, you look for the aircraft which is making it and which has not yet caught your eye. I hoped that if there were any prowling Messerschmitts around, we were low enough for our shadows to be at least partially hidden by the aircraft themselves. We came all the way home in perfect peace. However, some of the Audaxes were doing the same as us when, to their horror, an Mc110 sailed overhead at about 1,000 ft. There was nothing they could do, except to try and go even lower. It was not until the Messerschmitt floated serenely into the distance that they breathed again.

When we were nearing home, I decided to treat the camp to a low-level flyby-display, all five Gordons in close formation at about 50 to 100 feet. We had no radio, of course. For some time I had been making signs to the other pilots to get them well tucked-in to very close formation, and holding good position. I wondered, as I did so, why they were making such incomprehensible, peculiar and frenzied hand-signals back at me.

Soon I could see a knot of people standing in front of the duty-pilot's hut by the fence. They had obviously come out to see our return, and so I aimed to pass directly over them. I was just high enough for my right-hand wing-man to skim over the corner of the hangar-roof at the edge of the airfield. As I approached, I was surprised to see most of them running away in every direction, as fast as they could. Others were flinging themselves flat on the ground and some were standing as though transfixed. Flying Officer Osborne-Young, the instructor, remembers it distinctly. He was one of those who dropped flat on his face and prayed.

After landing, I discovered why I had caused such a fuss, and ended up having a very one-sided interview with The Butcher. On my Gordon was a 250lb bomb which had not left its rack. It was still under the wing and invisible to me – but seen horribly clearly, first by my wing-men and then by the spectators. One and all of them, being true professionals, knew full well that if a bomb-release wire had been tugged without success, and the bomb was still there – a hang-up – it might easily drop off at any moment later on.

There were only three more bombing raids by the Heinkels. Even so, they decreased in strength steadily, as Junck's resources dwindled, from three He111 bombers flyable on the 20th, to two on the 22nd and finally one alone on 26 May. Replenishment supplies were supposed to come the route of Athens-Rhodes-Aleppo-Mosul but, all along, their resources were too slender – on 26 May he had only four 50kg bombs left. German records confirm that from 20 May onwards, the serviceable Heinkels of the *Sonderkommando* were between two and zero. Further, this had only been achieved by extensive cannibalisation of serviceable bits from one machine to repair another.

Our camp was strafed by the Messerschmitts from time to time. They came in very fast from a shallow dive, made one pass, and away. Without radio or radar we were helpless. It was madly frustrating because we couldn't catch them, except on one occasion only.

After the loss of MacRobert at Mosul, we only had one remaining Hurricane. We put it up on standing-patrol, which is a desperately wasteful way of using fighters. However, we got it right, once. The pilot was at the right height, facing the right way, at the right time. He blasted one of the Messerschmitts out of its formation like a coconut knocked from its cup by a well-thrown ball at a fairground.

Although we had reduced the Iraqi Air Force effort to zero, and the Germans were by now no longer a serious threat, there were other problems to be faced. Being forced down, even uninjured, was not the end of the matter as we well knew. A pair of Audaxes on reconnaissance were intercepted by some Me110s and shot up. Fortunately they could both manage to glide down and make a safe landing on the desert. One pupil-gunner was already dead, but the two pilots and the other pupil-gunner were able to run clear before the Messerschmitts strafed the Audaxes and set them on fire.

One of the pilots and his gunner were taken to a local sheikh who befriended them and gave them each a cup of tea. As they were drinking it, an Iraqi policeman burst in, drew his revolver and shot them both out of hand. The pilot was killed outright but the gunner, though seriously wounded, had the presence of mind to feign death. After the policeman had gone, the sheikh sent him off to hospital. He survived to tell us the tale later.

The remaining pilot was surrounded by civilian Iraqis. Questioned after the campaign, they insisted that they were only going to take him prisoner. Unfortunately, they added, 'a man in the crowd' – whom nobody could remember or identify – had thrown a club at him. It had hit him on the head, killing him.

Just one survivor from four aircrew – although only one of them had actually been killed in battle.

One of John Hawtrey's Audaxes on patrol saw an Me110 forced-landed on the desert-plain behind Fallujah village. A Tiger Moth went out, found it and guided in two RAF armoured cars. He then landed alongside. Careful and prudent inspection showed it was not booby trapped, and so a salvage party was sent. They worked for two days, expecting to be attacked at any moment by the enemy, before towing it forty miles back into Habbaniya. We managed to make it serviceable after the campaign and it was flown away to Cairo. There it took part in mock dog-fights, to find comparisons and devise tactics for our own fighters. I had the excitement of doing some of those dog-fights later myself, in that same aircraft, over the Nile Delta. We had as much trouble keeping it serviceable as Junck did, and for the same reasons – lack of a spares supply.

German archives state that the Iraqis recaptured Fallujah bridge on 22 May – and lost it again on 23 May. I know that neither statement is true.

Mussolini also came into the picture, a bit later than the Germans. He said that the capture and development of Cyprus was key to the war situation. This would permit an Axis build-up through Syria. He would provide supplies. Between 19 May and 26 May, tri-motor Savoia 79s came to Mosul with rifles, machine-guns and other weapons for the Iraqis. Some more supplies of *matériel* were sent overland in trucks by the French, from Syria. To Junck's surprise, Baghdad ordered that all these arms were to be stockpiled in Mosul and Kirkuk – and that is where they went.

While the German situation was going from bad to worse, Dr Grobba was grossly overplaying his hand, claiming all was well. He forecast to Berlin that the Iraqis would continue to resist in the north of the country. In truth, they showed no signs of resisting anywhere.

By 23 May, Junck was very worried about Grobba and had completely lost confidence in him. He asked for a conference with General Jeschonnek in Athens. This, unfortunately and unknown to him, was just too late. Hitler, on 21 May, had already nominated Luftwaffe General Felmy to be Head of the German Military Mission in Iraq – the late von Blomberg's appointment.

On 23 May Hitler had signed 'Directive 30, Middle East'. This said:

> *The Arab Freedom Movement in the Middle East is our natural ally against England in the Middle East. …I have therefore decided to drive forward developments in the Middle East through the support of Iraq. The Military Mission under General Felmy will advise and support the Iraqi Armed Forces, and act as a control point for the direction of German leadership to Iraq.*

The Directive spelled out what would be done, and that which Hitler considered to be adequate involvement was:

> *…limited activity by the Luftwaffe* [which, besides its military activity,] *must reinforce the self-confidence and will to resist of the Iraqi Armed Forces and the people.*

In effect, more 'spine-stiffening' and not much else. The Directive also promised weapons deliveries from Syria.

Then Hitler, whether deliberately or unwittingly is not known, ditched *SonderkommandoJunck* (and Raschid Ali) by adding a strangling limitation to its effort. He said:

Whether and how the English position between the Mediterranean and the Persian Gulf will be brought to destruction will be decided only after Barbarossa.

After *Barbarossa*? After success in Russia? From that moment onwards, the German presence in Iraq was doomed.

By 25 May the balance of Habforce had finally clocked in. In the evening I attended a commanders' conference to plan the advance on Baghdad. A serious problem for the Army soon arose. They had no large-scale maps of the road and the scale of our flying maps was too small. Aircrew have to use small-scale maps because we cover large distances very quickly – if we had large scale maps, we would go from page to page so fast that it would take too much time to turn them all over.

The length of ground they wanted to be covered was a mere forty miles, from Fallujah across the desert to Khan-Nuqta, and thence through marshes and cultivation to the city. They needed to know how and where they could fan out either side. Naturally, the attacking army didn't wish to be restricted to marching or driving in a narrow line along a country road. That reluctance made great sense to me, for some weeks earlier we had caught the Iraqi Army, and its reinforcements, on that same narrow road, with devastating results.

I was sitting at a table by the door, listening and learning interestedly. Without much thought, I casually suggested that I could fly along their planned route next morning, taking a long series of photos all the way. From these we could lay down a long narrow photo-map of the road, and the area a mile to each side of it. I would then draw a grid on the map, with numbers and letters, and re-photograph it for quantity reproduction and issue to the army. It could become their home-made 'map' for the advance.

Some Army gunners quickly pointed out that it would be of no use to them. They opined, a little haughtily, that it might be perfectly adequate for transport, scouts and minute-to-minute forays, but it would not be precise enough to shoot from. I hoped that my face remained sufficiently grave, expressing interest at their comments, and that my true feelings were hidden. If as they suggested, the details shown, less than forty-eight hours old, were to be used only for checking recent flooding and for skirmishing, that was their affair. I offered that, as an ex-survey-pilot, I knew beyond question that my photographic strip-map would be far more accurate than any maps made from ground-surveys of twenty or thirty years before. Only the gunners remained sniffy about the idea, the rest of the audience was enthusiastic.

Next morning I waited for the sun to get well up so that shadows would be short and hide nothing. The longer I waited the less I liked the project, I wished it had never crossed my mind.

At last, we climbed into the camera-equipped Oxford with a pupil-rear-gunner, Aircraftman Smith – my pupil-navigator turned full-scale navigator-observer-camera-operator – and Frankie the dog. Up we went to 10,000ft which, if we were to cover a mile each side of the road, was the height made necessary by the only camera-lens we had available. The weather was wonderful and the smudge of Baghdad was just visible on the horizon fifty-five miles away. Smith and I together picked out Fallujah bridge and, snaking away to the east, the little dark thread which was the road to Khan-Nuqta and thence to Baghdad twenty miles beyond it. I nodded to him, and he lay down in the nose. I turned towards Fallujah and he began to give the corrections which would take me slap over the village and then along the road. Soon he said 'OK – steady – camera running. *Now.*'

I had nothing to do but fly with precision, eyes glued to the instruments for the levels and course required for survey-accuracy in the ensuing photographs. My aeroplane, an Oxford, was a lightly built machine, modified only for training and made of plywood and perspex. It had a single-barrelled .303in gun at the back, with no proper rear-turret, and no proper rear-gunner either. There was a curved bubble-windscreen in front whose shape would reflect the rays of the sun in almost every direction – potentially attracting unwelcome attention. Moreover, further attention-drawing shafts of sunlight were radiating from the circular bubble-canopy for my rear-gunner. On top of that, the whole contraption was painted, as were all training aircraft, a bright shiny yellow to be as noticeable as possible.

Feeling, in my mind, as inconspicuous as a lighthouse, this beacon-like device had to be flown dead straight and dead level for about twenty-five minutes, at 10,000 ft, on a gin-clear day – making itself an ideal target – with the crazy objective of ending up over an enemy defended airfield. If, as I feared, I was intercepted by a cannon-shell firing Me110, the fate of my little plywood aeroplane would be something like opening a box of wooden matches upside down.

As I have said many times, fear comes if there is the time and space to let it in. I had all the time in the world to work out how foul it was. I still look back on it as one of the most horrible things I have ever done – in parallel with trying to land an aircraft on a pitch black night with no lights.

I watched Khan-Nuqta, and then Baghdad, getting – oh so slowly – closer and closer. The Tigris and a railway came in from the left; the Euphrates was running away to my right; below, dark green marshes and fields – the supposed biblical site of the Garden of Eden. Would it never end? It seemed to go on for ever and ever.

At long last Smith said, 'Last photograph coming…NOW!' All three of us – pilot and two pupil-crewmen – felt strongly that we had been hanging around up there far too long. Only Frankie was unconcerned. 'Right,' I cried, 'grip tight!' and rolled the Oxford right over on to her back and in the same movement pulled the stick back to drag the nose down into an almost vertical dive. 'OK,' I thought, 'even if one of those sods sees me now while I'm like this, he'll have the bugger of a job to get me in his sights.' I watched the airspeed creeping up and up, making me feel better and better with every 10mph.

At 4,000ft there was a monumental explosion, followed instantly by a terrific blast of wind and debris flying all over the place. The thought flashed through my mind, 'Oh dear God, I've been hit and we are going to go straight into the deck'.

It took me an age – it seemed, but was probably all of five seconds – to work out what had happened. I had exceeded the aircraft's design limits and the air pressure had blown in the bomb-aimer's Plexiglas nose-window. The fragments flying around had been bits of perspex. Poor Smith, hanging on by his fingertips, was peering vertically down at damn-all. We pulled out gently, flattening out quite safely and happily at zero feet and wound our somewhat breezy way back to Habbaniya, keeping well clear of any habitations or information-posts. It was the only time that Frankie the dog did not stand squarely in the nose to watch over my approach and landing.

The photographs came out excellently. Helped by Smith, I spent the rest of the day, and most of the night, creating the original of the photo-strip map we had promised. The grid was drawn (to make it into a proper map) in the dawn of 27 May. The strip was then photographed, copied and issued on the same day, ready for the advance which was due to begin on the 28th.

Habforce set out from Fallujah and, it transpired later, our photo-maps proved very effective. There was practically no opposition beyond an odd skirmish and none of it caused delay. The School made only forty sorties. The army reached the outskirts of Baghdad the following evening – the 29th.

28 May was also the day that eleven Italian CR42 biplane fighters arrived in Kirkuk. Thank goodness they were too late to be put to really productive use. They were formidable machines, only slightly less effective than our Gladiators. More than effective enough, however, to seal the fate of any and every Oxford, Gordon or Audax they might have happened to meet up with. Fortunately, the only aircraft of ours that they encountered, near Baghdad on 29 May, was a 94 Squadron Gladiator flown by the CO, Squadron Leader Wrightman. He intercepted one of a pair and promptly shot it down. The other one escaped. His victim forced-landed near our army advancing on Baghdad and they took the pilot prisoner. He was unwounded, very confused and had practically no idea what was happening or even why he was there.

We were very lucky that Mussolini had not reacted in the very early days to Raschid Ali's pleas for support. It was not until towards the end of May – he was so often too late – that he put the excellent question to his German allies as to whether Iraq was to receive a real or only symbolic assistance. He was personally all in favour, he said, of a serious effort to support Arab sentiment against the British, and in this connection he also advocated the occupation by the Axis of Cyprus. Although his air force had made some contribution at the side of Junck, Mussolini received no very useful answers. Iraq was being abandoned totally. As for Cyprus, Hitler was clear that neither he could nor would justify the diversion of resources necessary to capture the island. If Mussolini pressed the idea, Hitler thought, he should be told to try it himself.

On the 30th, the School and Basrah worked together. Using locally produced 'screaming' bombs, we joined with 84 Squadron, 203 Squadron and 94 Squadron, making two heavy attacks on Raschid Airfield and Washash Barracks in Baghdad. The rooftop watchers of the Embassy had another grandstand view of our performance.

In the early hours of the 31st the Embassy reported that the Iraqis had requested safe-conduct for their flag of truce. Terms were negotiated during the day and communications between them and RAF Habbaniya were re-established. On 1 June Habbaniya was able to send a signal to Headquarters Middle East and to London on their behalf. Its exact text is in the official records, but the gist of it is given below:

June 1 – Reliably reported that Raschid Ali departed with 17,000 Dinars, about £17,000, said to be monthly pay of his troops. He was held up at Ba'quba and luggage searched when money was discovered and confiscated.

The general surrender appears due to disinclination to continue fighting after leaders had bolted, plus fear of our intensive bombing. Baghdad populace appear relieved and pleased to see British officers and civilians moving about the city again. Villagers on road Fallujah to Baghdad friendly. Only discordant note were people of Khadimain. Those north of that town show signs of fierce hatred, in keeping with their past record.

List obtained of Germans who stayed in Baghdad hotels. Of ten who arrived only four left, balance presumed to be casualties. Baghdad airport (Raschid airfield) being used today by RAF.

No flying school is staffed or equipped for warlike operations. The results achieved by No. 4 Service Flying Training School during the war in Iraq were remarkable. They, in 30 days, flew more than 1,600 sorties in old, slow and unsuitable aircraft. They dropped over 100 tons of bombs, including over 5,000 20-pounders. They fired 250,000 rounds of ammunition.

It was achieved through the determination and courage of the unseasoned instructors and also by the sheer guts of inexperienced pupils who took on any and every job. Supporting them were the ground crews, working under shell-fire in the heat of an Iraqi summer when metal parts of an aircraft get hot enough to blister the skin.

There were two sad events which occurred after our campaign ended. One concerned a stalwart friend of all the British in Iraq, and the other concerned a personal friend of mine.

Ambassador Knadenshue, and his wife, had extended American hospitality to a whole horde of British nationals and had gallantly kept them in their Embassy; protected, fed and with somewhere to sleep for a month. The Iraqis had demanded that they be handed over and the Ambassador had flatly refused. Pat Domville had also paid a visit from the British Embassy – and they wanted him, especially, because they saw him as 'a British Officer skulking in foreign territory.' Ambassador Knadenshue gave them short shrift on that one too.

He had done so much for us that our Embassy recommended, and our government agreed, that he should receive a British Order, or Decoration, in recognition of his unbounded help. However, the USA, at that time of the war, was still neutral – and strictly so. They flatly refused to let him accept any British award.

Undismayed, all the British nationals in Baghdad clubbed together to buy him a really nice 'thank you' present. It was a very splendid tea-and-dinner service in solid silver and suitably engraved. Our gratitude was both deep and sincere. Sadly, in the meantime Ambassador Knadenshue contracted a tetanus infection and had to be whisked off to hospital in Baghdad – and there he died, before his silver service could even be presented to him.

Mrs Knadenshue was an Irishwoman and she had never lived in, nor even been to the United States. She asked to return to her home in Ireland. The Irish Government refused to give her permission. She, they said, was an American citizen and that was where she should go.

Then occurred the only happy part of this sorry little tale. The Regent, Emir Abdulla Illah, whom the Knadenshues had rescued and driven in safety to Habbaniya before the campaign, stepped in to help. He awarded Mrs Knadenshue an Iraqi pension, large enough for her to rent a house and live comfortably in Baghdad. It continued till the end of the Second World War, when safe travel once again became possible and she could go home to Ireland.

The second sad event concerned that veteran of well over thirty bomber-missions, flown alongside me throughout the campaign – Frankie my dog. One evening, safely back in Cairo, he was snuggled beside me on the bench-seat of my rather elderly car, parked by the side of a road at the extreme southerly tip of Gezira Island. At my other side was the charming nursing sister from Habbaniya, who had come to Cairo for a few days leave. In front of us was a wonderful Middle Eastern moon, creating a sparkling, silvery, shining pathway across the Nile. Overhead were about a zillion flickering diamond-like stars.

Frankie showed an inclination to get out and I opened the door for him. Selfishly, I did not leave my girl and follow him to ensure he was all right. Moments later there was a squeal of tyres and a thump. Frankie was lying, struggling in the road. The car did not stop. We and a vet did all we could for him, but he died from dreadful internal injuries two days later.

Sixteen
Consequences

Around 28 May the unlucky Colonel Junck realised that the Iraqis, as allies, were past praying for and that his 'Heroic Gesture' was beyond recall. Neither he nor anyone else could save the day. He and his men packed up their goods and chattels – and *Doktor* Grobba from Baghdad too. He had finally come to the same conclusion as Junck. On 29 May, when our army was striding through the gates of Baghdad, they were leaving Mosul. Hitler ordered a last-ditch stand by General Felmy on 1 June, but changed that hopeless gesture on the 2nd to requiring the fighter defence of Aleppo. On 3 June they were all being withdrawn to Athens. By 10 June they were all gone, and both the Aleppo detachment and the Athens base had been closed.

In all, *SonderkommandoJunck* lost 21 aircraft: 7 Heinkel 111 bombers, 12 Messerschmitt 110 fighters, and 2 Junkers 52 transports, but the greatest loss of all was the loss of prestige and loss of face amongst the Arabs.

In the German texts there is a remark that their two flights of aircraft *might* have been able to cope on their own, alone, but not against the British air forces as well. This is a puzzling comment. If there had been no air-reaction on our side and no confrontation by the British Air Force, there would have been little or nothing for them to cope with. On the other hand, it might be because, written after it was all over, was a statement that we sent in air reinforcements of over 200 aircraft to build up a force which overwhelmed him. Bluntly, nothing like that number was ever there – 200 machines could not conceivably have been spared from the other campaigns. The German calculations must have added in those which were unarmed (like the Hart dual-control aircraft); the slow (80mph) and lumbering Valentias which remained far away at Basrah till quite late in the piece; the full strengths of squadrons tasked, rather than only the machines which reached us and we could use. Perhaps they even totted up some complete units based in India (such as 31 Squadron). We in Habbaniya counted only those which reached us and which fought for us. Those figures are in this book, drawn from the records of that time.

My personal view, as an old and experienced wartime operator, is that the real destroyer of Junck's *Sonderkommando* was the lack of proper and timely support from his own higher echelons, coupled with the lack of backing from the Iraqi armed forces. In spite of the Iraqi poltroons (and Grobba) Junck seems to have done a superlative 'best he could with what he had.'

That is not merely a shallow compliment from a combatant to a gallant opponent – I am supported by the writings of *Oberst* Dr Karl Gundenlach who headed the Luftwaffe Section of the Historical Research office. He could study and draw upon German wartime archives. Writing more than forty years after the event, he could be splendidly objective. He was, naturally, superbly placed to determine what various German operations were like, seen from the side of our one-time enemies. He has published several articles on the history of the Luftwaffe and in 1984 he contributed an article on the 1941 'War in Iraq'. Giving his considered opinion, he judges that although the German leadership met Iraqi requests for military assistance, they did it half-heartedly and inadequately. The German reactions were not planned ahead seriously, they were too little and too late. Then, even after the late entry, quick and powerful intervention would have saved the German position and won the full support of the Arabs. But, not enough was done by the German High Command to recoup the situation.

He further submits that the war in Iraq was in fact won by the British Air Force which utterly demoralised the Iraqi Army in the first few days. That is, when the School was fighting for its life, virtually by itself, and when our army was over 400 miles away. Then, he says, the RAF mopped up first the Iraqi Air Force, and then the German Air Force during the rest of the month

He concludes that Hitler threw away the chance of a substantial victory which could have been won comparatively cheaply. His careful analysis of the reasoning shows the conclusion to be sound.

At this point I wish to stop trying to communicate factual history in narrative form. I want to try and present, as incontrovertibly as I can, what would have been the most likely consequences if the School, entirely by itself, had not (as Karl Gundenlach says) utterly demoralised and defeated the Iraqi Army in those first five days – The Battle of Habbaniya. Inevitably it must hang from a bunch of fascinating 'ifs'. Let us begin with the situation before the battle.

Air Vice-Marshal Smart was following the policy set by Air Marshal Longmore and General Wavell, who had been pressing for political negotiation. Iraq was still ostensibly our ally and Raschid Ali was apparently seen only as a rebellious upstart. The Ambassador in Baghdad, Sir Basil Newton, with whom Smart was in close contact, was making light of Raschid Ali's intrigues. I found no records that the possible arrival of any German force onto Iraqi soil was known in Habbaniya until they appeared overhead. No wonder it is officially recorded that Smart was led to consider that capitulation to Raschid Ali's demands, which would be followed by negotiation was a logical and perhaps desirable course. The Commander in Chief, General Wavell, thought the same.

Behind that, and apparently unknown to our High Command, Raschid Ali on 18 April had undertaken categorically to give the Axis unrestricted use of *all* Iraqi airfields in exchange for their help. If the Germans had shown any positive moves to help in April (as they had promised to do, by letter ten days earlier, and as von Ribbentrop advocated strongly to Hitler) Raschid Ali could, and presumably would, have sent his tanks into Habbaniya to make good his undertaking. This he could have done, with complete impunity, at any time before 2 May. The overwhelming force was already on the spot before the end of April.

Nothing at Smart's disposal could have stopped a section of light-tanks driving up to his office and having their commander state his terms. In those circumstances, capitulation would have been inevitable. Then, beyond doubt, *if* the Germans had learned Raschid Ali's forces and armour were inside and controlling Habbaniya, the possibilities become fascinating to contemplate. There could have been a swift reaction, of which the Germans were entirely capable. Support by even a small and tough German airborne *kommando* in half-a-dozen transport-aircraft would have been ample. From my vivid memory, many of the elderly officers had no *will* to fight. Only our mixed-nationality ground forces had any kind of automatic weapons or grenades and, though brave, none of them were set up or trained for hand-to-hand conflict. The *Kommando* could have been in place several days before Kingcol had even begun its trip from Palestine on 11 May. *SonderkommandoJunck* itself might have landed at Habbaniya too, because our column did not arrive till 17 May, nearly two weeks later.

If the School had not immobilised the Iraqi besiegers in those first few days, the end result for Habbaniya would have been the same. Between 2 and 6 May, we could not have halted any attack by them, particularly if they had entered under cover of darkness. Neither our bombing nor anything else we had, air or ground, day or night, could in practice have kept them out.

Kingcol would then have had a wholly impossible task – to dislodge Germans (or Iraqis) in Habbaniya, with few guns and no armour. They would have had no administrative source for ammunition, food, or drinkable water, and no air-cover closer than Basrah or Amman, 300-400 miles away in either direction. The Iraqis' morale would have been high. Their forces outnumbered us by more than ten-to-one, and they had armour. Basrah, 300 miles south-west, had already said they could not render any land assistance, even if reinforced, because of flooding, and were talking of two years to dislodge the Iraqis, as in the First World War.

And what about Nasser's *coup* in Cairo, timed to coincide with the fall of Habbaniya? Kingcol's chances of recouping that situation, with or without the reinforcement of Habforce, would have been zero.

Gundenlach says '*substantial* victory missed.' How much did Hitler really miss by brushing aside Ribbentrop's advice and pressing on for *Barbarossa*?

In retrospect, the consequences of even a minor German presence in Iraq would have been quite disastrous for us. One of Britain's greatest men, Winston Churchill, Prime Minster at the time, wrote in his view of history[3].

The spirited defence of Habbaniya by the Training School was a prime factor in our success. The Germans had at their disposal an airborne force which would have given them Syria, Iraq and Persia, with their precious oil fields.

[3]Winston Churchill, *The Second World War*, Vol III, p.236, Cassells

Middle East oil-fields gone? Germans in control of Syria, Iraq and Persia? What might that have meant?

One may move to fascinating speculation on the damage to our image among the French, and the Turks. The political repercussions in those countries could have been most harowing for us. Having Germans, as a dominant power, sitting in a friendly Iraq just east of Vichy-controlled Syria, might well have moved the French to total co-operation with the Axis – to fight *against* the British; history records that, at the time, they were very close to it. Further, the Turks too might have crumbled, and co-operated wholly with the Germans. On top of that, in April the ordinary Arab was convinced that the British were done for; the Arab world, as Hitler hoped, might have risen against us. Whether these consequences would have been felt must, however, remain as speculation.

From pure speculation we can come down to what would have been hard facts *if* the School had not succeeded in preventing Germany obtaining a foothold in a friendly Iraq in May 1941. First, the enormously important Allied supply line from Teheran to Russia would have been severed. The denial of any Middle Eastern oil for us while they could take it all would have meant that our position in Egypt would become virtually untenable. We were alone in the war at that date and hanging on by our fingernails. America did not join us till after Pearl Harbor seven months later – 7 December 1941. Rommel was beating a path towards our main Middle East base, thus bringing German forces both east and west of us. Without British-controlled oil supplies in the theatre, it would have been impossible to build up our desert forces in the quantities needed by General Montgomery for his decisive battle in October 1942. He could not possibly have had his magnificent victory at Alamein. This is solid logic.

Move forwards from there. Develop the consequences of no Alamein victory. Rommel could not have been chased westwards across a thousand miles of desert. He, with his unhampered, powerful and seasoned *Afrika Korps* would have been free to defend Algeria. What odds would have been laid on the American North African landings of 1942 being successful? Even as it was, Monty came in behind him from the east and twice snatched General Bradley's unseasoned American forces out of a serious jam with the remains of his *Afrika Korps*. General Bradley himself made the caustic comment, in Algiers; 'My boys are like bananas – some are green, some are yellow, and they all smell.' Beyond that, could an American build-up, unsupported, have been good enough to open up and develop a Southern Front in Italy in 1943? Thus absorbing Rommel's forces which otherwise might have been used against the 1944 D-Day landings in France? Even with a European Southern Front in full swing, the first few days after D-Day were touch-and-go.

Finally, if the Germans had had unlimited Iraqi oil for their battles in Russia – what then? The chain of questions one can legitimately ask is remarkable.

The first turning point, or stepping stone, of the war in the west was the Battle of Britain in September 1940. Unequivocally, the second was the five-day Battle of Habbaniya in May 1941. The third was the Battle of Alamein in October 1942. The fourth was the American seaborne landing in North Africa in November 1942, because it became the launching pad for the Southern Front in Europe. None of those battles could have been successful without the success of the ones which went before.

The School's solo victory, from the air, over a well-armed force on the ground, reducing it to impotence and defying all military logic, is unique. Subsequent destruction of the local and more modern Iraqi Air Force, followed by the detachment of the German Luftwaffe, is not to be sniffed at either. Together, they avoided a potential disaster for the whole Allied war-effort. The Battle of Habbaniya is one of the most spectacular achievements of the Second World War.

The Commander-in-Chief, of all the Air Forces in the Middle East – British and subsequently the Americans too, was late Marshal of the RAF, Lord Tedder. He was the easiest of men to converse with. In 1943 I recalled the Habbaniya campaign, queried its total lack of publicity and asked his opinion of its importance to the Southern Front battles then being won. He thought for a few moments and said:

> *Well, it is a Royal Air Force epic. If the School had been overcome, the Germans would have got a foothold in Iraq. If they had then created a bridgehead behind us, through Vichy-controlled Syria from Greece, our Middle East base could have been nipped out with German forces both to its east and west. Certainly the whole course of the European war would have been changed drastically, if we had not lost it altogether.*

That we could have lost the war, had the Battle of Habbaniya not been won might be argued to be too grand a claim. On the other hand, maybe those thirty-nine pilots and their pupils really *did* save us? Naturally I am biased, but I have more than a suspicion that it might be true.

To me it is a pity that even after the battle, the Foreign Office, the Air Ministry and the War Office continued to refer to the whole affair as the Iraq Revolt, Raschid Ali's Rebellion, the Siege of Habbaniya, etc. I, together with all my living colleagues in the Training School were nonplussed as to why our achievement in winning this horrendous battle outright was never lauded in any way. I tried several times to find a reason and if possible a remedy. The affair was classed as a 'rebellion' or a 'revolt', which are, by definition, uprisings by civilians; only armies fight campaigns and battles. Or it was 'lifting a siege' – and a siege is not a battle. Also Iraq was politically our ally, and it is impolitic to fight one's ally. Hence, no campaign medal and no military or public recognition whatever *at the time*.

However, years later, for some reason which I have not unearthed, it became re-named 'The Campaign in Iraq', of which a part was 'The Battle of Habbaniya'. This made it possible for Squadrons and Army units which took part later on during the month-long campaign, to be duly and publicly recognised by the award of Battle Honours – to have 'Habbaniya' emblazoned upon their Standards – even though, in the span of those horrendous first five days when the actual and crucial battle itself was being fought, they took no part at all. A School, however, is not permitted to be formally designated an 'RAF Squadron', and only units variously defined as 'squadrons' may be awarded Standards and Honours. So for the School, fighting in fragile, self-modified, near-defenceless training machines and, *by itself*, utterly demoralising the entire Iraqi Army – nothing!

There is some recognition on the shelves of libraries, hidden from our country and the world, unpublished till 1953. This records:[4]

> *But no one who has studied the story of the Iraqi Revolt* [sic] *has forgotten, or is likely to forget, the achievements of No. 4 Flying Training School; for the rout of an organised army and air force by makeshift crews in training machines, who in less than a month flew some 1,400 sorties against the enemy, a feat unprecedented in the brief but crowded annals of air warfare. …in fact they were doing more than sustain a tradition. They were creating one.*

[4]Denis Richards, *The Royal Air Force,* HMSO, 1953

Epilogue

Anyone who was not in Habbaniya at the time cannot know what a dreadful experience it was. I have been unable to unearth the exact number of aircrew we lost, but of my own nineteen pilots who started the battle, ten did not see its end twenty-seven days later – dead, seriously wounded, or their nerves cracked and they had to be taken off flying. At the end of my 'rest from operational flying', my sleep over the month was calculated to have averaged out at two-and-a-bit hours per night. I too was 'proper poorly' like the others. The doctors sent me away for another, rather more restful, rest.

We, the minions at Habbaniya, never for a moment imagined that we were fighting a battle of strategic proportions. At the outset we believed we were tackling some Iraqi Army rebels. Later, to our concern, we came to the disturbing conclusion that some Germans had jumped on to the Iraqi bandwagon. Nevertheless at the end we judged that we, being truly British, had been tougher than they were and less easily scared off. So we had 'won'. We had no idea what we had really achieved.

The oil wells of Iraq and Persia were far simpler to reach than those of the Russians at Baku – if Germany had put her mind to it. It paid us to keep very quiet about it and, by the time the Americans had opened the Southern Front in Italy, our 'War in Iraq' had sunk without a ripple. New, exciting things were happening.

Sometime, during a short break in the proceedings, to let off steam, I rewrote 'The Instructor's Lament'. It was in 1941; please remember that was long before our Army and Air Force truly learned to work as one cohesive team – which did not come about till 1942, seventeen months later – the time of Alamein.

'What did you do in the War, Daddy?'
'I was hustled and ordered about,
Then everything cancelled and changed, Laddie,
I thought I was turned inside-out.'

'Bombed-up and started, then stopped, Laddie,
With never a chance to be lazy.
Stood-by and stood-down – and stood up, Laddie.
Headquarters was certainly crazy'

'Obsolete trainers to fly, Laddie,
With enemy guns on the hill
That covered the whole of the 'drome, Laddie,
And worked like a permanent pill.

'Guns, and no gunners to shoot, Laddie,
Bomb sights with no aimers to fly.
Night-flying without any flares, Laddie;
Not even a moon in the sky.

'Our army that didn't advance, Laddie.
We thought they were made out of wood.
Once dug in and watered, like plants, Laddie,
They seemed to grow roots where they stood.'

'I know that you think me a bore, Laddie,
I fear that you think me a fool…
If you take on a country at war, Laddie,
Please, don't take it on with a School!'

Acknowledgements

Most of the information within this book, barring my own vivid and sometimes debatable recollections, would normally have remained hidden from the world. I therefore express my sincere appreciation for access to the many sources of information (and their authors) which (and who) helped me in my paper chase, trying to find and sort out, as far as is possible, the true facts from all sides concerning this remarkable episode in the Second World War. Some information was recorded on paper, some on tape, some simply told to me by people who were there. They enabled me to knit together this account which is without question more complete and accurate than any existing official or unofficial record. With gratitude I would like to mention, particularly:

British

Air Marshal Sir John D'Albiac for his historical report *Ops in Iraq, 2-31 May 1941*, now part of the British wartime archives, Public Record Office

Air Commodore Henry Probert and his team in the Air Historical Branch of the Ministry of Defence (RAF)

The Search Department of the Public Record Office, London. In particular Official RAF Documents: Air 41/30, Air 29/554, Air 29/555, plus Appendices; *The Defence of Habbaniya*, AHB.II, J.3/2; *Ops in Iraq*, D'Albiac, AHB.II, J3/3; Squadron Records (F.540)

Several RAF Squadrons for access to their Squadron Histories

Air Marshal Sir Paul Holder, for his recollections of flying RAF Audax aircraft in the battle, of being shot down twice, and of his earlier work for Air Vice-Marshal Smart

Other RAF colleagues of that time, too many to be named individually, of different ranks who recounted their personal experiences, and gave permission to quote them

Major Rex Rice, who researched the names of attached pilots and the details of reinforcing aircraft

Mr Somerset de Chair, Intelligence Officer and official keeper of the War Diary for the rescue-column called Kingcol. He described its task in his book *The Golden Carpet*. Also, he most generously gave me his original copy of the photo-strip-map I made for Kingcol's advance into Baghdad

Lady Holman, whose husband Sir Adrian Holman was Councillor and Deputy to His Excellency our Ambassador in Baghdad. Her memories, recorded cassette tapes and written notes about the events were precise and invaluable

Dame Freya Stark, diarist and author of *Dust in the Lion's Paw* who included some useful material on the siege of the British Embassy, Baghdad, May 1941, describing events as though she had been in there at the time

The Foreign Office, Treaty of Alliance (1930) between Britain and Iraq

Mr F.H. Hinsley and his collaborators, for the book *British Intelligence in the Second World War*

Mrs Hugh Morgan, Mr Frank Norall and Mr John Bushell who translated and helped me with German texts

Mr Frank Wootton, President of the Guild of Aviation Artists. He decided to commemorate, with a painting, those who fought and were killed in the battle. It depicts a moment on the first morning. The original, presented to the RAF by Mr Victor Gauntlett, hangs in the Officers Mess of No. 4 Flying Training School. Mr Wootton most generously gave permission for it to be reproduced within this book

Iraqi

Iraqi Air Colonel Hofthi Aziz who attacked us in Italian-built Breda 65 fighters of the Iraqi Air Force at the time

American

Mr Floyd McGowin of Chapman, Alabama, who originally prodded me to research, in great detail, the material for this book, and then write it – 'before everyone has died'

The U.S.A.F. Staff College, Montgomery, and Flight Lieutenant Lawrence Haynes RAF, each of whom who put me in touch with several Germans, members of the Luftwaffe at the time. They, in turn directed me to material from the German wartime archives, unavailable from British sources

German

Oberst aD. Dr Kehrig, Director of the German Military Archives (*Bundesarchiv*, Freiburg) for his guidance through the record of *Der Krieg in Irak*, (123 pages – The War in Iraq) written by *Oberst* D Dr Bernd Philipp Schroder

Oberst aD. Dr Karl Gundenlach, Head of the Luftwaffe Section of the German wartime archives, for a mass of detailed facts

Oberstleutnant Gotz Adolf Stentzler who was flying Junkers 52 transports against us in Iraq at the time

Oberst Martin Drewes, later in South America. He flew Messerschmitt 110 fighters against us in Iraq